Mariana's Letters

Bien Vivre

Writings & Recipes

Mariana de Saint Phalle

Illustrations by Linda Low Wolcott

Editor Mimi Allen

Library of Congress Control Number:		2010914874
ISBN:	Hardcover	978-1-4535-9274-8
	Softcover	978-1-4535-9273-1
	Ebook	978-1-4535-9275-5

Mariana de Saint Phalle

E-mail: mdesp1@yahoo.com

This book was printed in the United States of America.

To order additional copies of this book, contact:
Xlibris Corporation
1-888-795-4274
www.Xlibris.com
Orders@Xlibris.com
86711

For Thibaut

Contents

Introduction

The sense that something is cooking on the stove or baking in the oven is an irresistible thing to investigate. To open the front door of your house and be enveloped by the unmistakable aroma of chicken roasting in the oven with all its accompanying herbal perfumes is the ultimate manifestation of well-being. That is why you learn to cook.

When I was young, Betty Jenkins came from Glasgow, Scotland, to run our kitchen. Her sister, Jean, came to run my sister and me. They raised us on things like rice pudding, oatmeal, brown betty, shepherd's pie and a Sunday roast with Yorkshire pudding. On Sundays, Betty would be stringing the beans through a stringer clamped to the kitchen counter while she listened on the radio to the Calvary Baptist church on West 57th Street with its immense choir and voluminous organ.

Thursday and Sunday would be maids' night out, at which time my mother and grandfather would take over to make exotic meals like pheasant, duck, venison, ris de veau or maybe an Indian curry with homemade curry powder.

Unfortunately, the Second World War came along and Betty and Jean went to New Jersey where they could make "good pay" on the assembly line.

Summers on Grandfather's island in Rangeley, Maine, would find Stella Quimby minding the giant wood burning stove. Her husband, Harold, was guide-handyman and their teenage daughter, Phyllis, who was madly in love with the good looking son of a local dairy farmer, was waitress. The best days were when Stella would let us help her make donuts. We got to fry the donut holes and after rolling them in granulated sugar we devoured them while still warm. In season, we were taken ashore by grandmother to pick wild blueberries in the fields, from which came Stella's blueberry pancakes, pies, and muffins. On picnics along the Dead River, we would gather birch sticks to make a fire so Grandfather could cook his morning catch of brookies, along with baby new potatoes.

During the war, we lived on the coast of Maine in the summer, and mother did the cooking. We lived mostly off our Victory Garden, Pollock caught off the dock and chickens from the local farm. We also had lobsters and dug for clams. A meal would be topped off with the best strawberry shortcake (not sponge cake) and thick whipped cream spooned from the bottle.

When I married, I was given two books by my mother, *Tante Marie's French Kitchen* and The *Dione Lucas Meat and Poultry Cookbook.* So I started out to learn French family cooking.

We lived on the north shore of Long Island where my in-laws had a bayman named Hawkins—a descendant of the famous Hawkins pirate family—living in one of their cottages with his family. His wife, Lillian, became my in-laws' cook and taught herself how to make the best chocolate soufflé I have ever had. She would set the soufflé in a pie plate with just a little hot water and place it in the lower third of the oven. This made a soufflé that was cooked on top but was nice and gooey on the bottom.

Later on, I married in to a very old French family where I really came to love the everyday home cooking that is served *en famille.* Most entertaining is done within the extended family. Recipes are passed down to brides in handwritten notebooks and go with the brides to their husband's home. This is a bit like what happened with Catherine de Medici who, when she married the king of France, arrived with all her Italian recipes and the chefs to cook them. Chateaux have favorite family recipes and ours is Lapin á Cudot, a rabbit casserole which is always better the second day. Although our family comes from Champagne, we spent a lot of time in the south of France in the valley of the Luberon where the cooking is Provencal.

While living in Washington D.C. for a number of years, I began to write periodic newsletters which I would send to anyone who requested one. They were titled *Mariana's Letter,* and later, *Dining In.* Because I come from a family of writers, I was excited at the thought of writing my own letter in which I planned to talk about food and offer recipes, but also tell stories, some true and some not. This book is the product of all those letters and the great support I have had from my readers.

Everyone is a potential cook either by necessity or pleasure. It is just a matter of observing what is going into the pot to make it a good soup. Most of us pick up cooking along the way in life, starting as a child licking the bowl of chocolate icing.

Letter # 1

JANUARY, 1984

The Belgian Embassy residence in Washington D.C. is housed in one of the lovelier mansions of the city and has the added distinction of having fine cuisine. A while ago, when the ambassador's wife brought a new young chef over from Europe, it prompted some culinary buzz on Embassy Row.

So it was with delight that one day I accepted an invitation to a cooking demonstration in the embassy kitchen. As in many old houses, the kitchen was below ground level, in the basement to be precise. What I found there was a simple kitchen by American standards. The modest square room had white-tiled walls, floors and counters. There was a noticeable absence of any but the most essential equipment—there were no gadgets. In this simple workplace, elegant breakfasts, luncheons, dinners and receptions were prepared daily. The young chef had only one assistant, his wife. The secret, of course, was organization. As I watched, each ingredient was carefully measured out, chopped, or sliced and reserved in ordinary glass custard cups. The work area was then put in order so that the final preparation could proceed without interruption. A Japanese sushi bar employs exactly the same method. You will find that you save time, avoid omissions and produce a better result if all the ingredients are measured and prepared first.

Professional kitchens are often very small and have several chefs working at the same time. This demands a minimum of clutter, careful planning of each task and equipment that is easily accessible, preferably hanging or on open shelves. A busy chef cannot afford to spend time opening a lot of cabinet doors. An efficient kitchen should be of simple design, totally washable (consider tiled walls) and uncluttered. Remove non-essential, seldom-used utensils and store these away from the main work areas. What is important is to have the finest stove and ovens you can afford, a selection of fine knives, good quality cookware, rather than great quality, a generous refrigerator-freezer, a top-of-the-line food mixer and processor, and by all means a good scale. If you have ever carried your kitchen in a backpack or prepared a meal in a boat's galley, you know much can be done with a minimum of tools and space.

A good practice is to go through your kitchen and remove all those wonderful pieces of equipment that you have not used in the last year and cut down on the clutter that invariably results from culinary buying sprees.

Carre d'Agneau Gratiné au Poivre Vert
Belgian Embassy (Rack of Lamb)

Ingredients:

A rack of lamb for four persons (separated into chops and tied back together)

A bouquet garni of chopped celery, onion, garlic and carrots left loose

¼ pound butter

2 tablespoons of walnut oil

For the Sauce:

½ tablespoon tomato paste

1 tablespoon of flour

½ cup of dry wine

½ cup of water or stock

Preheat oven to 400°F.

Melt 2 tablespoons of butter and 2 tablespoons of walnut oil. Add the rack of lamb and brown on both sides. Add the loose bouquet garni and roast in the preheated oven for about fifteen minutes; the meat should be pinkish-red inside. Place the meat on a heated platter and keep in a warm place. Pour off the excess fat in the pan and let the bouquet garni brown a bit over a medium flame. Add the ½ tablespoon of tomato paste and let it color a bit. Sprinkle the flour over and stir well with a flat wire whisk if you have one. Add the white wine and continue stirring until smooth. Add the water or stock and let the sauce cook a minute until thickened. You can omit the flour if you prefer. Add salt to taste and strain into a small saucepan.

Mix the following ingredients together in a food processor and spread over the meat:

3 slices of bread

2 tablespoons of parsley

1 slice of onion

1 clove of garlic

1 tablespoon of green peppercorns—optional

1 tablespoon of pine cuts (pignoli)

Just before serving, sprinkle 2 tablespoons of grated parmesan or gruyère cheese over the top of the lamb and let it brown under the broiler. Reheat the sauce and pass it separately. Accompany with some lovely fresh green beans or Dauphinoise potatoes for a perfect main course.

Food for Good Measure

As you probably know, most chefs never travel without their knives; it is a tradition of their profession and they treat their knives with great care. Chef Jean Louis at the Watergate in Washington, D.C., also traveled with his balance scale, which lived in an impressive leather case. He considered it essential. Why? Because that is the only really accurate way to measure. For example, cake flour weighs 5.2 ounces per cup unsifted and 3.3 ounces sifted. The texture of a cake can be affected by the use of flours of different density and whether they were measured before sifting or after. This cannot happen if the flour is weighed rather than measured. The secret to consistency, then, is to record a recipe in weights. This is very important when it is necessary to double a recipe; no adjustments are necessary. To double a recipe successfully, follow the original recipe, first measuring and then weighing and recording the weights for future reference. Since weight is affected by density, there is a difference between chopping, mincing or grating, and between liquid and dry. So, when the book says 4 ounces of flour, measure, weigh and record for future accuracy.

When baking bread, be guided by its consistency as you knead it, since 6 cups of one type of flour can mean 6 ½ of another: another example of the advantage of weight measurement. Darker flours rise less, so there must be a certain amount of white flour added if you want a light loaf. Pumpernickel is a typical heavy loaf. Another note concerning flour: use pastry flour in cookie recipes so the cookies will retain their shape. Don't forget to line the lightly oiled baking sheet with wax paper.

Croissant Critique

Les Grands Moulins de Paris is a century-old French company that supplies flour for the bakers of France. It has now founded a subsidiary company in the United States called Vie de France, which started its career in Vienna, Virginia, selling croissants baked fresh every day to stores and restaurants—along with long loaves of French bread, petits pains and baguettes. Its campaign to popularize the croissant in America has met with considerable success.

An interesting thing has happened: the American croissant is often superior to its French counterpart. Why? Flour, like wine, varies around the world and even within sections of countries; so the flour that is used determines to a great extent the character of the finished product. Vie de France shops for the right flour for its products all over this country and Canada. The North American breadbasket stretches all the way from Manitoba, Canada, to Texas, an expanse of latitude yielding a wide selection of grains. Since this represents an enormous area with very divergent weather patterns and soils, it is possible to find a grain producing flour suited to a particular purpose. For example, very good hard flour comes from Minnesota, whereas lovely fine pastry flour can be found in Illinois. Since the grain fields in European countries are concentrated in smaller areas, the choice is much narrower. Pastry chefs from Europe coming to work in the United States are impressed and delighted with the variety and quality of American flour at their disposal.

Croissants are only good when very fresh, so if you are not going to use them the day they are bought, freeze them, even just overnight. At breakfast time remove them from their wrapping and place in a preheated 350°F oven on a piece of foil and set the timer for just seven minutes. The same rule holds true for baguettes, petits pains, etc. Heating a hard roll wrapped in foil steams it, making the crust too soft. When preparing croissant sandwiches, remember they can be split and filled more easily if only partially defrosted. Use a serrated knife. After filling they will be ready for eating in half an hour.

Fair Game

I was introduced to the joys of waterfowl and upland game by my grandfather who would bring his limit from the marshes of eastern Long Island to my mother's apartment in New York City, where they were hung by their necks (neither plucked nor drawn) from a grating outside my bedroom window, eight floors above the street. Lying in bed at night I could not help but see their dangling silhouettes swaying gently in the evening air before I drifted off to less-than-sweet dreams. Hanging breaks down the tough fibers in the bird's flesh and after a few days also produces a rich, distinctive flavor. Freezing also breaks down the cellular structure of the meat and is more practical than hanging, but I do not think you get quite the same flavor. Certainly it will be less gamey.

More than once the elevator man knocked on the front door informing my mother that someone living across the way was complaining of the view and the odor and was about to call the police and the department of health. After several days it would be decided that the ducks or birds were ripe enough and a grand dinner would take place with very specially selected guests and wine. Wild rice was always on the menu and the breasts were served very, very pink.

The breast meat of the duck is the best for eating, so one duck serves two persons. Remember that waterfowl and upland game have no fat on them, so you must provide the moisture in the preparation. Today, America is a wonderfully rich source of game, due not only to its native varieties but also to its immigrants: Hungarian partridges, chukar partridges from the Himalayas and Chinese pheasants (now indigenous to the northwestern central states). In the category of bigger game we have Russian boar in parts of Tennessee. If you feel you have eaten a fair assortment of feathered game, visit France in the shooting season—the variety in the Paris butcher shops is enviable. Once at a shoot in the Loire our day's rewards were handsomely laid out in the old chateau courtyard and, in addition to the hares, rabbits and pheasants, there were pigeons, blue jays and even sparrows. The rule of the shoot was that anything that walked, ran or flew was fair game, but also everything shot must be edible.

Our family has always liked to cook pheasant and duck in a covered casserole, so that the bird bastes itself. If roasting, place on a rack upside down until the last few minutes. Pheasant is served with a bread sauce. Casseroles with rich cream sauces tend to hide the lovely delicate gamey flavor. Keeping in mind the need to retain moisture as you cook the bird, if it is young use high heat for the shortest duration possible until the bird has reached the desired doneness. Older birds, however, respond better to stewing. A cardinal rule with game birds: do not overcook!

Quail La Galleria

This deliciously simple method of preparing quail comes from a small Italian restaurant in Frankfurt, Germany, which includes this dish along with its very good Italian menu when fresh quail are available.

Fill the cavities with salt, pepper and a generous helping of sage and roast in a very hot oven for twenty minutes using a heavy ovenproof frying pan. I suggest rubbing the birds with oil or butter before roasting. Now the interesting part: after you remove the quail from the oven the minute the bell goes off, pour over them well-reduced chicken stock (1 cup for the two birds should do) and simmer the birds gently, turning often for just five minutes and serve immediately. Scrape all the wonderful juice from the bottom of the pan to pour over the meat. I found that the game birds were brown and succulent at the same time. If you use this method with a little larger bird, split the bird first and increase the roasting time. (I increased it by ten minutes for partridge.)

Bread Sauce

This recipe from the *The Gourmet Cookbook*, Volume I (published by *Gourmet Magazine*), is a very good accompaniment to roast game:

Stud an onion with 2 cloves and put in a saucepan with 2 cups of regular milk. Add cayenne and salt to taste. Bring to a boil and let it boil five minutes and then strain. Add about 1 cup of fresh bread crumbs (easy to make in a food processor) or enough to thicken the milk.

Correct the seasoning with salt. For a richer sauce add some butter or cream at the end. 1 cup of preserved gooseberries may be heated, drained and added to the finished sauce. Carrots would be a good choice of vegetable to serve both for color and taste.

Pheasant Pressure Cooked

Put the pheasant in a pressure cooker and add one can of consommé and time for twelve minutes. Remove the pheasant and place under the broiler for three to five minutes for browning.

If you do not have a pressure cooker, gently simmer the bird for one hour and then put under the broiler. You then also have the beginnings of a wonderful stock to which you can add the carcass later.

Since you will not have drippings, prepare a velouté sauce with tarragon using the stock, or serve the bread sauce.

Pheasants Meadow Farm

The following recipes are from Francis and Susie Low of Easton, Maryland, who not only are known for their experience in shooting upland game but also for what they do with it when they get back to their kitchens.

Here is a recipe for those with a dinner to give and pheasants to spare. A day or two ahead, cook several pheasants, saving the drippings, and make croquettes with the meat, reserving some of the dark meat for later use. Refrigerate. On the day of the dinner, cook the remaining pheasants, carve off the breast meat and arrange down the center of the platter. Surround with the croquettes which have been deep fried while the pheasant is cooking. Garnish with parsley and then pass the reheated sauce separately. Serve with wild rice or pureed chestnuts.

Tips

The 4-inch square gauze bandages, when taken apart, make good bouquet garni wrappers.

When following a recipe you can use two to three times the amount of fresh herb rather than dried.

Quote

"Verro, the learned librarian, tells us that the number of guests at a Roman dinner was ordinarily three or nine—as many as the graces, no more than the muses. Among the Greeks, there were sometimes seven diners, in honor of Pallas. The sterile number seven was consecrated to the goddess of wisdom, as a symbol of her virginity. But the Greeks especially liked the number six because it is round. Plato favored the number twenty-eight in honor of Phoebe, who runs her course in twenty-eight days. The Emperor Verro wanted twelve guests at his table in honor of Jupiter, which takes twelve years to revolve around the sun. Augustus, under whose reign women began to take their place in Roman society, habitually had twelve men and twelve women, in honor of the twelve gods and goddesses. In France, any number except thirteen is good."

—Alexandre Dumas, *Dictionary of Cuisine*

Letter # 2

WINTER, 1984

I have developed a cheese soufflé for two persons, because the cookbooks always seem to assume there will be four for dinner.

A soufflé can be totally prepared up to two hours in advance and placed in the refrigerator. Remove twenty minutes before baking and add a little time in the oven to compensate for the cold dish.

Cheese Soufflé for Two

Ingredients (serves 2):

2 tablespoons of butter

1 tablespoon of butter to grease dish

2 tablespoons of flour

3 very fresh eggs (extra large)

1 extra egg white

¾ cup milk warmed

Nutmeg, cayenne, white pepper, salt

¾ cup grated gruyère cheese (or a mixture of cheeses)

Grated parmesan

Melt the 2 tablespoons of butter slowly in a saucepan and put the third to soften in a 4-cup soufflé dish. When the butter is melted, remove from the heat and stir in the 2 tablespoons of flour. When the mixture is smooth, return the pan to the heat, stirring all the time for a minute or so. Remove the pan from the heat again and add all the warm milk, stirring until smooth. Return to the heat and stir while it thickens a couple of minutes. Remove from the heat and immediately add the egg yokes, one at a time, leaving the whites in a mixing bowl along with the one extra egg white and a little salt. Add all the seasonings to the roux and set aside. All the above steps can be done well ahead of time.

Set the oven rack in the middle position and the temperature to 400°F. If the roux has cooled off too much, reheat it to tepid. Beat the egg whites until stiff and then thoroughly fold one third of them into the roux. Then add the grated cheese, and finally fold in the remaining egg whites lightly but completely. Pour the mixture into the soufflé dish. If you have some, sprinkle grated parmesan on the top and place in the oven for twenty to twenty-five minutes. Serve at once, dividing the portions with two forks.

Some Thoughts on Starting a Wine Cellar

If one is to be interested in good food, one should also be interested in the wine to be served with a carefully-prepared meal. As the king of chefs, Brillat-Savarin put it in 1825, "A meal without wine is like a day without sunshine." So from time to time, I will give you some thoughts on wines. The first step is obviously to start a wine cellar, so let me pass on to you a few thoughts.

If you are starting your wine cellar from scratch, concentrate on quantity rather than quality. Enjoyment of wine is solely a matter of personal taste. The best way to learn about wines is to buy as many bottles as your budget will allow, but only one of each. Sample them, reject those you don't enjoy and buy those you like. Learn to read the label: it will tell you all you need to know. If buying French wines, concentrate on the years rather than the name of the producer. Lesser-known vineyards in a great year will produce far better wines than the well-known Chateaux of a bad year. In wine, as in art, people are too frequently paying for a bad bottle with a well-known name rather than a great year from an unknown Estate. Much later we will talk about wine futures. My 1970s, bought for $5.00 in 1970, are now worth as much as $200 a bottle. A well selected 50 bottles will give you a great start to learn what you enjoy and what wine goes with what kind of food.

As I write this, we are celebrating George Washington's birthday. The father of our country knew little of inflation. In running for office in Virginia in 1776, he hosted the voters of Frederick, VA, with 13 ½ gallons of wine at a cost of $0.56 a gallon.

What's New

Champagne served with an ice cube to replace white wine as an aperitif. Any pasta served simply with a light coating of very good olive oil and grated parmesan. Mimosas are gaining more and more of the Bloody Mary crowd. At the Carlyle Hotel in New York, a split of champagne is brought to the table with a pitcher of fresh orange juice for Sunday brunch.

Baby new potatoes boiled in their skins until done but not soft, cooled and split in half lengthwise and topped with a little sour cream and caviar. This is an effortless hors d'oeuvre and looks very attractive made with golden caviar from the west coast.

Sherried Olives

Combine all the ingredients listed below and marinate for three or four days, shaking the bottle every so often.

Ingredients:

1 jar (7 ½ ounces) pitted medium black olives and 1 jar the same size of pitted green olives

3 cups olive oil

1 cup sherry

1 cup sherry vinegar

1 small garlic clove smashed

1 small red onion cut into medium rings

1 tablespoon thyme

Drain at serving time and reserve the marinade for another batch.

Tuna Fish Sandwiches

Marian Burros recently ran a story in the *New York Times* on tuna fish sandwiches. The most elegant one consisted of white-meat tuna, mixed with curry, raisins, Dijon mustard, chopped onions and mayonnaise on dark bread.

Letter # 3

SPRING, 1984

While some people may look for the first pale greening of the willow weeping over a cold rushing stream of awakening trout, or the first forsythia forced into bloom in a sunny window, I watch for the first shad roe to enter the markets.

Spring brings new, fresh menus with ingredients that are riper and not so travel weary. So here is a dinner built around shad roe to celebrate the change of seasons in a culinary way. You are given a palette of spring colors for eye appeal: the bright green asparagus coupled with the earth-colored little potatoes and the red strawberries in their puree. Lime sherbet is a lovely alternative to the whole strawberries.

Menu for a Spring Dinner

Large California asparagus

Baby new potatoes, steamed in their jackets

California strawberries with strawberry puree and cassis

I reprint here a few helpful facts on the preparation of shad roe from *The Encyclopedia of Fish Cookery* by Albert Jules McClane (Henry Holt and Company). Fresh shad roe should stand in ice-cold salted water for five minutes and then be very gently simmered for only a few minutes until it just firms. It can be completely cooked in this manner if it is to be used in certain dishes where it be chopped, such as scrambled eggs or soufflés. If the roe is to be served whole, this procedure makes it solid and easier to handle when sautéing. It also prevents bursting—a common problem. The roe should be cooled before proceeding with any recipe. When baking or broiling, pre-simmering is not necessary, since the membrane has no direct contact with the heat source. Never prick the roe, as it tends to become dry in the cooking.

Another point to remember is that the price of shad roe declines as the season progresses, so when it becomes relatively inexpensive, stock your freezer. Shad roe freezes extremely well in a freezer-weight plastic bag half filled with water.

Shad Roe Amandine

Ingredients (serves 2):

1 pair shad roe

½ cup dry bread crumbs (fresh crumbs dried for a few minutes in the oven are the best)

¼ cup peanut oil

Salt and pepper

¼ cup of milk

¼ cup of flour

2 tablespoons lemon juice

½ cup almonds, blanched and slivered

Chopped parsley

Separate the pair of roe very carefully with scissors, so as not to tear the membrane. Prepare roe as stated in general directions above and cool. Season with salt and pepper and dip in the milk, then in the flour, then in the milk again and finally in the bread crumbs. Sauté gently in the oil until brown and just a little pink inside. This only takes a few minutes. Remove to warm plates and sprinkle with lemon juice. Pour the oil off the pan, add butter and sauté the almonds until brown; pour over roes and serve sprinkled with chopped parsley. This recipe is also good for shad filets.

Baby Potatoes Steamed in Their Jackets

Wash potatoes. Steam in a strainer, covered and placed over boiling water until done. Stir in fresh chopped parsley and serve. You will find that this method of cooking the potatoes requires a little more time but will give superior texture and flavor. They can be prepared in advance and reheated over steaming water.

Asparagus

Asparagus is one of the only vegetables where bigger is better. It is important, though, that you choose stalks of equal size. Break the stems where they tend to snap off naturally and neaten the broken edges. If you like, scrape the stalks with a vegetable peeler under cold water and store in a pan of cold water until ready to cook. Drop them one by one in a shallow pan of boiling water so the water keeps its temperature and cover. Cook until just tender and remove. Wrap the stalks in a linen towel on a plate to keep warm. It is not necessary to accompany them with a sauce unless you want to, since they are so luxurious in their natural state or with just a little lemon butter.

For many years Passy was a very popular restaurant in New York City. Their clients would look forward to the first giant California asparagus arriving on the menu. The restaurant knew how to cook them to perfection, and the asparagus would arrive ceremoniously at the table in bright green mounds on big silver platters lined with linen towels. It was truly a feast for the eyes as well as the palate.

Strawberries with Strawberry Puree Cassis

The important thing to look for when buying strawberries is ripeness for flavor. Yellowish strawberries—no matter how large—will be tasteless. Stem, rinse, dry on toweling and combine with a sauce of pureed strawberries, fine-grained sugar and cassis to taste. Store in a glass bowl in the refrigerator until serving time. If you wish, sprinkle the top at the last minute with slivered almonds (if you have not used them on the shad roe.)

I am including two other recipes for shad roe, as they are too delicious to remain unmentioned. The first is very easy, since you can now buy sheets of phyllo dough in the frozen food department at most supermarkets. The second recipe, using either fresh or leftover roe, is marvelous for breakfast or a light luncheon.

Shad Roe in Phyllo

Ingredients (serves 4):

2 pairs of fresh shad roe

4 thin slices of bacon

Lemon juice

Salt and pepper to taste

16 sheets of phyllo dough

½ cup melted sweet butter

(Note: Phyllo dough must be defrosted in the refrigerator overnight and then kept at room temperature for two hours.)

With scissors, separate each pair of roe in two pieces very gently, so as not to break the membrane. Salt each piece and wrap with a slice of bacon. Sprinkle with lemon juice and pepper.

On a wooden board, layer four sheets of phyllo dough, brushing melted butter between each layer. Place one roe near a narrow end of the dough and bring the end flap over the roe. Now fold the long ends toward the middle, encasing the roe, and brush the flaps with melted butter. Finish rolling up the dough. Repeat with the remaining roes. Refrigerate the rolls for an hour, or if you are in a hurry, put them in the freezer for a short time. Bake at 350°F until just a nice light brown. Do not over-bake, as the roe should be pink in the center.

Shad Roe, Supreme Meadow Farm

Ingredients (serves 2):

1 pair of shad roe, either leftover or simmered gently until done

2 tablespoons butter

Heavy cream

Eggs, smallest possible

Toast

Fresh dill

Remove any casing from the roe. Melt 2 tablespoons of butter in a double boiler and add the roe, breaking it up with a fork. Add cream to make a thick hash, and warm thoroughly. Season with salt and pepper. Poach the smallest eggs you can find, such as pheasant, quail or the smallest size domestic. Spoon the hash on large toast rounds. Top with the poached eggs and chopped fresh dill. Don't forget to poach your eggs in water with a little white vinegar and to remove them with a slotted spoon onto the hash or paper toweling if they must wait a few minutes. They can be poached ahead and dropped for a minute in simmering water to reheat. Do not overcook—the yolks should be runny.

Mustard

In the fourth century, Palladius wrote down a recipe for making mustard which closely resembles mustards of today; and even before him in 42 A.D. another Greek writer wrote down a smooth mustard sauce. But it was the city of Dijon that restored these old recipes and made again the mustard that is so much a part of French cooking today. The Dijonnais started making their mustards in the thirteenth century. In 1752 a vinegar maker named Maille became purveyor to Madame de Pompadour and took the title of Vinegar Distiller to the king of France and emperors of Russia and Germany. He made over one hundred table vinegars and twenty-four varieties of mustard. Both the Maille and Dijon mustards are still available today.

Mustard is a wonderful flavoring to add to your vinaigrette dressing, to spread on a steak when it is done, and to a coq au vin or boeuf bourguignonne. It is wonderful mixed in tuna fish salad and to baste meats while cooking. The following is an absolutely delicious recipe from *The Taste of France* by Robert Freson (Stewart, Tabori and Chang Publishers) that produces a roast chicken of the must beautiful golden color.

Poussin á la Moutarde

Ingredients (serves 2):

1 very small whole chicken, a fryer

2 to 3 tablespoons Dijon mustard

½ cup crème fraîche or heavy cream

Salt

Freshly ground pepper

1 tablespoon butter

Preheat oven to 425°F.

Truss the chicken and coat it with a thick layer of mustard.

Bake in a small gratin dish until the mustard turns golden brown, about forty minutes.

Heat the crème fraîche in a small pan. Take the chicken out of the oven and remove any surplus mustard; pour on the crème fraîche. Bake for ten minutes.

Place the chicken on a deep warm platter: whisk the sauce left in the gratin dish and taste it for seasoning. Whisk in the butter. Pour over the chicken just before serving.

Letter # 4

SUMMER, 1984

Flying in High Style

Flying in high style means taking your dinner with you. It is not any fun to dine poorly en route. On my last flight to Europe on a 747, I noted the time from take-off until the first food or cocktail was offered—a long two and a half hours. Now, since most transatlantic flights leave between six and eight in the evening, that means cocktails and dinner start sometime around nine-thirty, and many times the cocktail arrives with or after the dinner tray. Also, the dinner itself can be unappealing. It is much more fun to have your own lovely party—so pack a picnic and start your trip on a high note.

Due to the proliferation of sophisticated take-out stores, a very tasty meal can be put together, well packed in solid containers the day of the flight. Look for dishes that taste good at room temperature. Keep cutting with a knife to a minimum.

Be extravagant, as this is a party, but keep the menu light. The book *Overcoming Jet Lag* by Dr. Charles F. Ehret and Lynne Waller Scanion (Berkley) has a very interesting program which was used by President Reagan on his trip to China last year. It really does work. The book recommends a high carbohydrate dinner for those wishing to relax and sleep later. Dine at eight and retire with your eye shades by ten. There is a bonus in that you end up at your destination with a picnic bag ready to put in the car or to serve a delicious little meal à deux in your hotel room after a tiring day.

> "I get no kick from champagne,
> Flying so high with some guy in the sky
> Is my idea of nothing to do,
> But I get a kick out of you."
> —Cole Porter

I recently took a round-trip flight at midday on US Air and am happy to report that they served a very attractive lunch on a well-designed tray. There were two choices for the meal: a truly rare roast beef sandwich on a very good roll with fresh fruit for dessert or a cannelloni, which I ordered on the return flight and which was equally good and perfect for luncheon. The stewardess told me that Marriott is the caterer, but that US Air personnel supervise all the menu selections and preparations to ensure the same standards of quality on all their flights. It is so nice to see an airline making an effort to serve a light, fresh meal.

In the Bag (For Two)

1 soft canvas bag for the picnic (can be packed flat later)

1 corkscrew and bottle opener

2 each of knives, forks, spoons, in a zip lock bag

2 no-iron dish towels for napkins

1 no-iron dish towel to cover picnic

2 light-weight plastic plates (preferably with rims)

2 flat-bottom old fashioned glasses (unbreakable)

Hand wipes

1 serrated knife

Salt and pepper grinders (very small are available)

Plastic bags for dirty dishes

It is very helpful to pack a light plastic reusable tablecloth in your suitcase for those happy picnics along the way. It serves as a combination ground cloth and tablecloth and can be purchased at most supermarkets.

A Sample Menu

Caviar or smoked salmon

Toast-like cracker or a hard roll

A chicken entrée that tastes good at room temperature

Rice or pasta salad

Seedless grapes

A good cheese

A very good piece of chocolate (a truffle)

One of the ultimate in entrées for an airplane picnic was enjoyed by Inge and Bill Witter of New York, who had birds they had just shot in Columbia, South America, cleaned, cooked and wrapped to be eaten still warm on the flight home.

Picnics along the Way

The first thing to do in the morning is to study your road map to look for rivers or streams that cross your route, since they provide a pretty place to relax. Second thing: When in Europe, buy your lunch by eleven o' clock as most European shops close promptly at noon for up to three hours. Here is a typical menu that is always procurable:

Fresh baguette

Local cheese, olives

Saucisson, a local pâté or other cold meats

Fresh fruit

Bottled water

Local wine

In the majority of towns the boulangerie (bakery) is located near the church, so look for a church spire. If you happen to arrive on market day, you will be able to buy a real midday feast.

The effort spent in assembling the necessary picnic equipment will, I guarantee, pay off handsomely in the pleasure you will find in each day's "Dejeuner sur l'Herbe."

> "I never travel without my diary. One should always have something sensational to read in the train."
> *The Importance of Being Earnest,* Act I.
> —Oscar Wilde

As you may recall from an earlier newsletter, one of the loveliest books about food is *Foods of Italy* by Guiliano Bugiallis (Stewart, Tabori and Chang Publishers). I recently spent a day listening to and watching Mr. Bulgiallis execute a menu of recipes from his book. It was a real extravaganza, as this amusing man sent four student helpers from l' Academie de Cuisine in Bethesda, Maryland, scurrying around in a whirlwind of tasks in the tiny demonstration kitchen. Wonderfully useful bits of information were dropped like peas on the attentive audience between kneading pasta dough, preparing tomato sauces and sipping wine. I will pass some of these tidbits on to you from notes I took.

On Italian Cooking

The difference between the cooking of northern, central and southern Italy is not in the use of different recipes, but simply in the substitution of ingredients for ones which are native to the particular area. So in the north, butter is substituted for oil, as oil is produced in the central and southern regions and not in the north. Bologna, on the border of north and central Italy, uses a combination of vegetable oil and butter. Florence uses oil, and the south does consider deep frying in oil. The name of the recipe remains the same. The same preparation techniques are followed, but it is the substitution of ingredients that creates the subtle taste differences in each locale.

Dried Beans

Add 1 tablespoon of flour to the soaking water of dried beans to cut down the soaking time by four to five hours. The same method can be applied to hard-skinned fresh-shelled peas. Leave them one hour in the same solution, which will soften the outer skin so that the inside and outside cook evenly and quickly. If your peas are a bit too mature, also add a bit of sugar to the cooking water.

Basil

Do not freeze basil for winter use. Instead preserve the leaves in olive oil, filling the jar only three-quarters full, as the leaves expand threefold. There will be a small change in color. For recipes calling for fresh basil but not oil, preserve the basil in between layers of coarse salt, having the top and bottom layers salt. The color will remain good. When the basil is processed with a mortar and pestle and coarse-grained salt, it retains its color. If you are chopping basil with a knife, add a few leaves of fresh, dark spinach (which has no taste) for a good green color, as the basil will darken.

Preparing Vegetables

Store vegetables to be used in a recipe in a bowl of cold water. Remove, chop, dice or whatever, and return to a fresh bowl of cold water. You will find this preserves the fresh taste of the legumes. Do the same thing with fresh shrimp, but add a little salt to the water.

Separating an Egg

The best way to separate an egg completely is to crack it and pour it into your hand, letting the whites drain into a bowl through your fingers, while rolling the yoke gently until it is completely cleaned of the white. It goes very quickly.

On Dough

If your kitchen seems too warm for rolling out dough, place the dough between two sheets of plastic wrap and roll it quickly on a cold surface, such as marble or formica.

When you are preparing pasta dough, roll it out on wood so it will breathe, not on a non-porous surface. When folding dough to run it through a pasta machine, be careful not to flour the top, as it will not adhere when folded in three (like an envelope) to fit the machine.

A Pasta Dough

Ingredients:

½ cup of unseasoned bread crumbs, preferably homemade and finely ground

3 ½ cups unbleached all-purpose flour

1 cup lukewarm water (for the dough)

Pinch of salt

Soak the bread crumbs in a small bowl of lukewarm water for fifteen minutes. Drain the bread crumbs, discard the water and squeeze as dry as possible in your hand. Place the flour on a board and make a well in the center. Put all the ingredients in the well and gradually incorporate the flour, scraping the bottom of the well with a fork. Knead until smooth and then process in your pasta machine to a thickness of one-sixteenth of an inch. Cut into one-and-one-half inch squares and boil in course-salted water for one to three minutes, then drain. Sprinkle with 8 tablespoons freshly grated parmigiano and serve immediately.

Fresh homemade pasta can be stored in plastic bags for five to six days outside the refrigerator, so is a wonderful item to take camping or on a boat.

Homemade pasta—Cook two minutes. It is soft and light, so use with light sauces.

Dry pasta—Cook twelve to fifteen minutes. It should have a bite to it. Supports heavy, peppery, full sauces.

Store-bought fresh pasta—Falls in between the other two.

Artichokes

Artichokes—low in calories, high in vitamin and mineral content—are at their very best in April and May. An artichoke's size does not determine the quality or maturity of the vegetable. First and foremost, the leaves should be tightly packed; do not choose the ones that have started to open. Pick the bright green ones. In winter and early spring the tips of the leaves can have a bronze tint, which will produce an excellent flavor. Artichokes can be stored for up to two weeks in the refrigerator. Do not wash them before storing, just sprinkle with a few drops of water and seal in a plastic bag until ready to use.

To prepare, rinse the artichokes under cold water, pull off the stem and two layers of the bottom leaves and cut the points off the remaining leaves. Place in a pot just large enough to stand them in, add two to three inches of boiling water along with a little lemon juice, a little salt and a few drops of oil to make the leaves shiny. Cover and boil gently for thirty to forty-five minutes. Lift out the artichokes and drain them upside down before removing the center choke with a metal spoon. If you want to cook them in the microwave, place four artichokes in a glass casserole upside down with ½ cup of water, 4 lemon slices and 1 tablespoon of vegetable oil. Cook them covered at high power, rotating them twice, for sixteen minutes. Remove them from the oven, turn them right side up, recover and let stand for five minutes. I am very fond of using them for picnics, especially since they do not need chilling.

The Little Things Count

In a recent interview in *Gourmet* magazine, George Lang, the owner of Café des Artistes, which was on New York's Central Park West, remarked that most restaurants minimize the importance of the basic little things which will set the tone of the meal. He goes on to say that the customer is often not aware if the bread, butter and coffee are excellent, but will notice if they are bad. That is certainly true. I am sure that we have all been served stale bread and weak coffee at some very pretentious restaurants.

Ideas

Plan a dinner the week you are going to put your summer annuals in the garden. They will look wonderful arranged in all kinds of containers with moss or bark, or whatever, used to hide the plastic containers or even flats.

The Georgetown Club Salmon Tátare

Ingredients (serves 10):

1 pound cleaned boned fresh salmon

For the sauce:

¼ to ½ medium onion, finely chopped

3 tablespoons finely chopped parsley

2 tablespoons small capers

2 tablespoons Dijon mustard

1 tablespoon olive oil

Juice of ½ lemon

Salt and pepper to taste

Combine the sauce ingredients and store in the refrigerator. Just before serving, finely chop the salmon by hand (not in a machine) and add the sauce. The dressing can be made ahead, but the salmon should be chopped at the last minute and combined with the dressing just before serving so the color will stay bright pink. Arrange the salmon on bib lettuce leaves and garnish with toast points, extra chopped onion and capers.

Salmon and Avocado Café des Artistes

Fill ½ of an avocado with coarsely chopped very fresh raw salmon and garnish with caviar.

Sauman Mariné Au Lime—French Embassy, Washington

Ingredients:

Salt and pepper

Paper-thin slices of salmon to cover the plates

½ lime

1 tablespoon olive oil

Bread—dense homemade or toasted white

Sprinkle a small plate with a little salt and pepper. Arrange the paper-thin slices of salmon on the plate. Salt and pepper it lightly again and squeeze ½ of a lime over the salmon. Drizzle 1 tablespoon of olive oil over and let rest a minute before serving. Serve with attractively sliced bread.

Flowering Herbs

In the late spring lovely lavender flowers blossom in your chive bed. Separate the flowers into miniscule flowerets for garnishing soups, salads or any dish where chives might be used. Aside from the fact that the color is dramatic, they impart a very delicate chive taste and are a little crunchy. Later on in the summer you can use calendula petals, which taste a little like saffron. Nasturtiums make a good addition to salads and rice pilaf.

Next month we will begin a summer series on cooking and eating outdoors, at the beach, on the terrace, on a boat and other summer places.

Letter # 5

LATE SUMMER, 1984

Summer is a time for eating out—by the sea or by a stream in a field, parked at a campsite or even on your own balcony or terrace. A summer meal cooked and consumed outside is a culinary challenge undertaken annually with great expectations by greater and lesser cooks alike—a back-to-basics phenomenon that arrives with the ants and mosquitos each summer.

A note about preparing meat: before grilling, trim as much extra fat as possible from any type of meat while it is still cold. Do not remove it from the refrigerator or cooler earlier than necessary, or you will lose most of the juices to the platter. If the meat is frozen, thaw it about seventy-five percent to hold the juices and to keep the interior pink during cooking.

Hamburgers

Hamburgers are not passé. They can be superb if seasoned and cooked properly. Noted food critic and author, James Beard, states in *Delights and Prejudices* (Atheneum) that his mother often served hamburgers at their famous summer beach picnics near the Columbia River in Oregon. Mrs. Beard believed that a hamburger tastes much better cooked on a griddle set on the grate over the fire, rather than putting the meat directly on the grill. First, she seasoned prime lean ground beef with finely chopped onions, available herbs, garlic, salt and pepper. Then she formed the meat into rather thick cakes and placed them on the hot griddle. Another delicious Beard hamburger (Napa Valley hamburger) calls for 1 pound ground steak, 1 tablespoon onion juice, 2 tablespoons of heavy cream, salt and pepper. Again, make a rather thick cake.

Grilling Lamb

When grilling lamb, season generously with garlic slivers inserted in the meat before grilling. Also try basting the lamb with a mixture of butter and/or oil with a little white wine and some freshly chopped tarragon. Mr. Beard suggests in his book that dill is a wonderful substitute for tarragon on a lamb.

Last summer we spit-roasted a baby lamb (slaughtered the day before) over a birch fire at our camp in the Rangeley Lake region of Maine. Every ten minutes someone gave a quarter turn to our home-designed spit (since we have no electricity there) until the color and smell told us it was done. Beforehand, the lamb had been spread with a mixture of oil, Dijon mustard, salt, pepper and a lot of crushed dried rosemary. We continued to baste it with each turn. It was superb eating for twenty people, with the bone going to the golden retriever.

Clams

Clams—littleneck or cherrystone—are synonymous with summer and the shore and are a wonderful course for an outdoor dinner from the grill.

Steamed Clams or Oysters from the Grill

6 clams per person

A square of heavy-duty foil enough to wrap 6 clams

1 tablespoon of butter per package, creamed with minced parsley and scallions, lemon juice and pepper

Seal the packages completely, but leave air space inside.

Place the package on the grill over hot coals for about ten minutes or just until the clams open. Remove the packages to plates or soup dishes and open. Mop up the wonderful broth inside with French bread after you've eaten the clams.

Another way to cook shellfish: when the coals are right for a steak, place oysters or clams on the grill and then cover them with a water-soaked burlap bag until they just start to open. Remove and dip in melted butter.

Grilled Halibut

Try grilling halibut in a wire basket placed in the grill.

Serve with a hollandaise sauce flavored with lime juice and topped with a demitasse spoon of caviar. Another tasty sauce for fish is butter creamed with lemon juice, thyme and a little Dijon mustard.

Baked Potatoes from the Grill

To serve the world's best baked potatoes, bake them for half an hour at 400°F in the oven and then transfer them immediately to the grill, letting them bake until soft inside (about half an hour). Turn them occasionally while the rest of the dinner is cooking. The outsides will be burned but the insides will be as fluffy as whipped potatoes and the flavor is unbeatable!

I am including an easy and dependable hollandaise sauce to accompany summer dishes.

Blender Hollandaise Sauce

Put 4 egg yokes, 2 tablespoons lemon juice and a pinch of cayenne in the blender. Cover and turn the motor on low. Remove the cover and gradually add 1 cup (2 sticks) bubbling hot butter in a steady stream. When all the butter has been added, turn off the motor and either serve immediately, refrigerate or freeze. Reheat in a bowl or double boiler over, not in, simmering water. Hollandaise does not have to be served any hotter than warm.

Lime Hollandaise

Omit the cayenne, reduce the lemon juice to 1 tablespoon and add 2 tablespoons of lime juice, 1 teaspoon of lime zest and drops of Tabasco to taste.

By the Clock

The other day I read the ultimate timed-menu article that started three days ahead for a dinner at six. By the time the final hour was at hand before the guests would arrive the preparation time remaining had been reduced, in theory, to just minutes. It was exhausting reading, but what I found a little odd was the allocation of just ten minutes for setting the table for this glorious meal.

In ten minutes you hardly have the time to count the napkins and plates, much less the time to make your table look worthy of a day's work. Pleasing the eye always improves the taste of the dinner.

If you are planning a dinner party, fix your table during a quiet time the night before, a task that has the advantage of letting you see how your table will look at night.

Fresh Fruit Sherbets

The following recipe for fresh sherbet is from the Four Seasons Restaurant in New York (www.fourseasonsrestaurant.com). There is no comparison between this and the store-bought. The colors and flavors are so refreshing and they would be a lovely finish to a hot night's meal.

Strawberry Sherbet

Ingredients (makes 1 quart):

1 pint strawberry puree (3 pints strawberries)

1 ½ pints simple syrup (see below)

Juice of 2 lemons

Hull and puree the fruit in a blender or processor. Add the simple syrup and lemon juice. Check to be sure it is not too tart or too sweet. Pour the mixture into the container of an electric ice cream freezer and run for twenty minutes.

Note: Freeze a sample for the first time. If it is too icy, add a little more syrup; if it is too soft, add a little water.

Simple Syrup

Bring 2 cups water and 1 cup sugar to a boil and cook for 5 minutes. Cool.

Other Flavors

Raspberry—3 pints raspberries

Pear—8 pears peeled and poached

Peach—10 peaches peeled and poached

Substitute 1 pint of juice for the puree in the following:

Orange—10 to twelve of the best juiced oranges

Lime—27 limes

Lemons—14 lemons (omit lemons in the basic recipe)

The restaurant also likes to make a parfait using a tall glass with layers of sherbet and stiffly whipped cream.

Garnish with the fruit you have been using.

Cheese Cake

This recipe for cheesecake is from Doris Geary of Pomfret, Connecticut, and is a great favorite with everyone who has been lucky enough to eat it. It should be made the day before it is served.

For the Crust:

1 eight-inch spring-form cake pan, buttered lightly

24 single graham crackers (crushed with a rolling pin)

Approximately ¼ pound melted butter with 2 tablespoons of sugar and 1 teaspoon cinnamon to bind and to your taste.

Preheat oven to 350°F.

Blend ingredients and press into pan with a rubber spatula.

Bake six minutes and cool. Leave the oven on.

For the Filling:

4 eight-ounce packages cream cheese at room temperature

4 regular size eggs

1 ¾ cups sugar

1 ½ teaspoons vanilla

Mix all ingredients in a food processor or by hand and pour into the pie shell. Bake for eighteen minutes. Cool one hour.

For the Topping:

1 large carton sour cream

2 tablespoons vanilla

1 tablespoon sugar

1 teaspoon cinnamon

Mix sour cream and vanilla and pour over the cake.

Sprinkle with cinnamon and sugar mixture and bake six minutes at 350°F. Cool before placing in the refrigerator for ten hours or more.

Tips from Thibaut: Wine Labels

The most important information on a wine label is, of course, the year. Also informative is to see whether the label designates the wine as château bottled, if a Bordeaux, or domaine bottled, if a Burgundy. If the label is marked with the name of a *negociant*, it necessarily means it will be a mixture, but still within the designated locality. The importance here is to know the reputation of the dealer. Above all, know the words *Appellation Controlée*, a French guarantee of the area of production and the quantity that the producer is allowed to market.

—Thibaut de Saint Phalle

Letter # 6

FALL, 1984

Preparing a meal on board a boat is a matter of dealing with the smallness of the galley and the largeness of the appetites. Sailing cooks over the years have developed some ingenious ways to make life in the galley quite delightful and the meals more varied and delicious. Experts from Mrs. William F. Buckley to Pierre Franey have written articles on how to cope afloat. In southern waters a good rum punch near at hand certainly does help one cope, and champagne does the same in the Mediterranean. I am speaking from over thirty years of galley (slave, they used to call it) service as I write these notes. These same ideas can be easily applied to rustically-equipped summer cottages and campsites.

First, if you are going to use canned goods, buy only the best product available to make a palatable dish. Secondly, find out beforehand what fresh foods are going to be available en route. I learned the hard way about the availability of food when sailing along the southern Turkish coast a couple of years ago. The skipper, my friend, and the first mate, my husband, had carefully placed three cases of wine bottle by bottle in the bilge the length of the main cabin, their contribution to stowing the boat. The wives were given a couple of hours to navigate the markets on the island of Rhodes in order to provide three meals a day for ten days. My experts told me that there would be plenty of fish to buy fresh from the fishing boats, as well as local bread, cheese, fruit and vegetables.

Off we sailed in the afternoon and through the night to find the coast of Turkey, and I am using the word 'find' as it seems appropriate from the conversations held by flashlight over charts in the cockpit late at night. My first and remaining impression of the Turkish coast is no sound, no movement, no fishing and no boats. This is a sea without birds, which could only mean a sea without fish—and for the cook that is a catastrophe. The waters had been fished out by the Turks using dynamite to bring up the catch. The villages were so poor that they rarely saw an egg, much less any quantity of fruits and vegetables.

Bread and cigarettes were plentiful, however. There was, for us, an enormous language problem, especially at the Customs House. We flew the Greek and French flags from Rhodes until we approached the Turkish coast, when we smartly lowered the Greek and replaced it with the Turkish (or else we might still be there).

Our captain went ashore to the Customs House in order to clear our boat for the return trip. After two hours he returned, having given away all the boxes of cigarettes we had brought with us for this purpose, but to no avail—there was no stamp on our papers. Something else had to be done to gain our shore clearance. Our ever resourceful men went back ashore to the Customs House with copies of Playboy tucked under their arms. Two hours went by, the time it took for every man in the town to see the magazines, after which our papers were stamped. We set sail late in the afternoon with a full moon promising to light our way back to fruits, vegetables and fish. (It took a while, as our men got us to the right island but not to the right harbor.)

Stowing the Galley

A cooked Virginia ham can be hung by its bag in a shady place on the boat and thinly sliced for lunch or dinner. Tasty and well-packed ones can be ordered from S. Wallace Edwards and Sons, at www.virginiatraditions. com. In the same family of meats, whole hard salami is delicious and can also be hung in a cool place. Think of the foods that are eaten in the hot countries, as they are often foods that do not spoil easily: mustards, pickles, anchovies, sardines, olives, nuts, citrus fruits, rice and pastas, canned beans and tomatoes.

For a simple salad using unrefrigerated ingredients, take a can of red kidney beans, heat to lukewarm and drain. While still warm add oil, vinegar, chopped raw onions, thin slices of salami sausage and chopped parsley. Another salad is Pan Bagnia (basically the ingredients of Salade Niçoise), which consists of stoned black olives, green or red sweet peppers, anchovies, lettuce, tomatoes and cold cooked string beans. Arrange whatever you have of the above on 2 halves of French rolls cut lengthwise. Then pour a little olive oil and vinegar over the rolls, join the 2 halves together and put them under a heavy weight for half an hour. There, you have a nice lunch for a hot day.

In an article for *SAIL* magazine, Pierre Franey wrote about galley equipment. Not how much equipment, but what equipment, makes the difference. He suggests: 3 good knives for paring, boning and slicing bread, and 2 chef's knives for other duties. He also likes to have a 10-inch casserole, a Dutch oven and saucepans that nest into each other. For the latter, I suggest the Cuisinart Stowaway, a nice commercial cookware set.

Following are some summer salads.

Tomato Charente

Slice ripe tomatoes that are at room temperature and substitute cognac for the vinegar and then add olive oil, salt and pepper.

Salade Niçoise

Cube and boil potatoes until just done. Drain well and while still warm pour a little vinaigrette dressing over them and set aside. Line a glass bowl with Boston or Bibb lettuce leaves and layer the rest of the ingredients in the following order: The reserved potatoes, cooked, fresh, whole small string beans; well-drained chunky white tuna broken apart with two forks. Finally, garnish with pitted black olives, tomato wedges, anchovy filets and a well-seasoned vinaigrette dressing.

Salade Niçoise makes a nice luncheon served with a light Italian wine and country bread, followed by fruit and cheese.

Lemon Rice Salad

Ingredients (serves 10 to 12):

3 tablespoons unsalted butter

2 cups uncooked long-grain rice

4 cups boiling water and salt

2 large lemons

2 cups green seedless grapes, sliced in half lengthwise

Heat the butter in a 3-quart saucepan over medium heat. Add the rice and cook, stirring constantly, for two to three minutes or until the rice becomes opaque. Stir in the boiling water and add salt to taste. When the liquid returns to the boil, cover the pan, reduce the heat to low and cook for eighteen minutes. Do not stir.

Remove the pan from the heat. Uncover, place two kitchen towels over the pot, replace the lid over the towels and let stand for twenty minutes.

Fluff the rice with 2 forks and transfer to 3-quart serving dish. Cover with a towel and let stand for thirty minutes. Meanwhile, grate the rind of the lemons and combine the halved grapes and ½ the lemon juice; let stand for thirty minutes.

Add the reserved lemon rind and the remaining lemon juice to the rice and toss. Add the grapes with the lemon juice and toss again.

Outdoor Table Setting

The most impractical, overused and expensive tableware is disposable paper and plastic, because you end up with a large bag of trash. Plastic and paper blow away as soon as a light breeze stirs and bends or slides around on your lap during cutting. It is not difficult to wash reusable equipment in a stream or bucket of salt water. Prell shampoo works well in cold and salt water and comes in a little plastic tube to keep in the picnic basket. Also, large drip-dry napkins stay on your lap, do not blow away to litter the countryside and can be washed and dried quickly in a sunny spot.

Herbal Hints

Now that fresh herbs are in season everywhere, I am including a small list of the most-often-called-for herbs and their uses taken from some information sent by HERBS NOW!, a fresh herb and vegetable wholesaler.

Basil—Has a sweet vegetable flavor. Use with tomatoes, zucchini, eggplant, squash, carrots, beans, soups, stews, poultry and seafood dishes. It is a traditional Italian ingredient. Also: dips, egg dishes, or to top a baked potato.

Bay Leaves—Strong flavor of the leaf (not edible) mellows with cooking. Remove leaf before serving. Good with soups, stews, stuffing, poultry, game, and fish dishes, tomato-based dishes. Flavor vinegar and marinades and cooking liquid for chicken or seafood.

Tarragon—Sweet-savory flavor used often in French cuisine and in tartar and béarnaise sauces. Uses: carrots, squash, onions, beans, potatoes, beets, poultry, and fish dishes, and mayonnaise-based salads.

Thyme—Slightly spicy. Used often in Creole cooking and to stuff meats, poultry, fish or seafood. Other uses: mixed with cottage cheese, tomatoes, potatoes, beans, peas, carrots, spinach, and turnips.

Letter # 7

LATE FALL 1984

Bless the average American kitchen: it is a marvel, a joy to come home to. Not only is an array of mechanical time savers available, but the room itself is generally bright and welcoming and an obviously important place in the home, regardless of size. We have tended to update and upgrade the importance of the kitchen with the demise of live-in help, a trend not followed as much in older houses of France and Italy, where stoves and refrigerators are often small and the lighting is poor.

I cannot resist citing a couple of rather extreme examples of old European kitchens, the first in a lovely old château situated on a low hill in the Nivernais two hours south of Paris. To my mind château can be male or female. They can be proud, arrogant, gracious, gloomy, cheerful, introverted, fat, thin, short, or tall. This particular one was an aging lady with gracious rooms and long windows gazing at the fields lying below. Since there was a light rain falling, we took the inside route down a very long old corridor behind the dining room, which was really like going back two hundred years by just stepping through a door. First came a small room where children were playing, then followed a simple laundry room and then a large archway through the kitchen.

Like the others, this room was cool and dark and of stone with a high and vaulted ceiling. The center space was occupied by a large sturdy table in front of which stood an enormous smiling Moroccan chef wearing a gleaming white apron and a little cap on his head. It was a mannish, ancient kitchen where progress had feared to tread, perhaps because the château was last restored in the eighteenth century.

A short drive led to our next friend, a princess who lives in a male, thin, Victorian, Peter Arno-type château. She is one of seven princesses, daughters of an Austrian-Belgian prince who now sits tall and thin on his tall, thin horse up high on the living room wall. The prince had told his daughters that they must only marry princes, nothing less, a difficult task after the war when there were so few left. The sister princesses "settled" for counts or spinsterhood, one even taking over the barns to become a cattle agent and sell French Charolais to the Kleburg ranch in Texas and the cattle barons of Brazil. Our hostess disappeared for a few minutes and we could hear her footsteps echoing off the bare floors as she passed from room to room. She soon returned bearing a lovely silver tray with champagne glasses, and we sat on a rainy afternoon sipping our drinks and talking of the past in a room that could easily hold one hundred guests and seven little princesses.

The third kitchen was in a fifteenth-century Tuscan castle whose lands had held one hundred and forty tenant farmers for hundreds of years, until the only remaining widow recently left to follow her children to the city. The Castelo di Spannocchia is owned by Count Ferdinand Cinelli, who divides his time between Grosse Point, Michigan, and Tuscany. The castle is now a foundation used by archeological students during the summer. Architectural students are learning the techniques of restoration by modernizing the old buildings on the property. The castle's kitchen is in an enormous semi-cellar half above the ground and half below. This kitchen is presided over by a cheerful local Italian chef who feeds thirty to sixty people three times a day from a vaulted room equipped with an eight-burner stove and a very small dishwasher. A stone sink and table complete his workplace. For many years two women came down from the nearest hill town for the summer to cook on a little four-burner gas stove of about 1920 vintage. They refused to cook on the new eight-burner stove, saying they were accustomed to their old little stove, and they turned around and walked back to their village. I was amused to see the chef make his own lunch, a simple pan bagnia of horizontally sliced Italian bread coated with homemade olive oil and fresh ruby red herbed tomato puree.

July in Tuscany is caper season, when they are harvested, dried on plates for a day or two and then bottled in vinegar to age. Capers are flower buds of a plant that grows only in the cracks of old walls. If left to bloom, the bud becomes a pretty white flower.

Paris Notes

Lunch at a simple café in Paris offered poached filet of sole on a bed of stewed rhubarb with a drop of vanilla added and a little tomato coulis poured on top for color.

The centerpiece at family meals is often a covered soup tureen filled with thick slices of fresh baguettes, self-serve, of course.

A Beautiful Cucumber Soup

The charming young wife of a French embassy official parted with the recipe for a delicious and eye-appealing cold soup. It is the garnish that makes it so special.

Cucumber Soup with Garnish

Ingredients (serves 6):

3 cucumbers peeled and seeded (or seedless cucumbers)

1 garlic clove

1 cup chicken broth

3 cups sour cream and a little crème fraîche, if available

3 tablespoons white vinegar

2 tablespoons salt

Parsley

Combine all above ingredients in a blender and chill.

Garnish:

2 tomatoes peeled to release the seeds and juice, then chopped into small cubes

Thinly sliced almonds sautéed in butter until just slightly brown

Chopped fresh tarragon

Finely chopped chives

At serving time ladle the cold soup into soup plates and sprinkle the garnish over each serving.

To peel a tomato, immerse in a pot of boiling water just a minute until the skin starts to crack, then remove with a 2-pronged fork and peel.

A Hot Weather Drink

There used to be a very well respected fishing and shooting club on Long Island's south shore (about an hour's drive from New York City) called The Southside Club. Well known for its trout, pheasant and duck, it was equally renowned for inventing the Southside, a drink made with either rum or vodka. The drink's popularity has spread to other club bars, each with its variation. The main difference is whether the ingredients are shaken in a container with ice or whipped in a blender, which gives a fine froth and minces the mint.

Take your choice—either way it is a truly refreshing cocktail.

Southside (per drink)

¾ glass lemon juice sweetened with simple syrup

1 ½ jiggers Mount Gay rum or unflavored vodka

Generous amount fresh mint leaves, finely chopped (if you are not using a blender)

Shake or blend. Pour into an old-fashioned glass with ice and a mint sprig and add a dash of club soda.

Preparing Fresh Vegetables

With irresistible farm stands and our own lovingly-cared-for vegetable beds, it is important to pick or buy vegetables at just the right moment for size and freshness. Emery Stein of Potomac, Maryland, raises fine French string beans which she picks just before dinner and displays still in the basket to her guests before she cooks the beans ever so slightly for the meal. What a treat! Vegetables can be blanched for a couple of minutes, rinsed in cold water to stop the cooking and then stored in the refrigerator for later use. At meal time simply sauté them in butter and fresh herbs.

A Show Stopper

My mother's best friend was Rachel Smith from Boston. As children they spent the long summers together visiting back and forth between their families' camps on Rangeley Lake in northern Maine. When Rachel grew up her parents took her on a grand tour of Europe, where at dinner one night she was seated next to a dashing young German Count. He followed her back to Boston, they were married and went to live on a thirty-thousand acre estate in what became East Germany after World War II. She once told me that to add a festive note to her summer parties she would place her largest goblets on the dinner table. Just before the guests sat down, fresh peaches would be washed, peeled or not, and pricked all over with a fork and placed in the goblets. When everyone was seated, very cold champagne would be poured over the peaches, and at the end of the meal dessert plates would be set down and the now delicious champagne peach would be taken from its glass and eaten washed down with the peach champagne. I would suggest the addition of a little vanilla ice cream.

What Do You Do with All the Shells?

Human nature seems to encourage us to pick up pretty shells and driftwood on beaches and carry them all home, but I have always wondered what happens to the marine artifacts then. Are they discarded, stored away in an old shoe box or simply left aging in some corner of the beach house porch? Shells can be a valuable addition to a table setting, especially if you can collect on a beach that has some good-sized and nicely bleached shells. Even whitened clam shells are useful. I use the smaller ones as individual butter dishes on a summer table; larger ones can hold appetizers, dip, candles, sugar, salt or pepper. A group can be arranged as a centerpiece mixed with non-wilting greens or simply placed in a glass bowl. Large, flat green leaves make attractive doilies on plates or hors d'oeuvre trays. Queen Ann's lace, that lovely chalky weed that grows along the roadside, looks perfect when combined in an arrangement with shells . . . and it doesn't cost anything but a little time.

A View from the Terrace

Half an hour before guests are coming for dinner on the terrace, hose all the foliage where bees and mosquitoes like to live. The cold water has a tendency to put them to sleep. Cool water will also bring down the temperature on a hot night and make everything look fresh.

Letter # 8

LATE FALL 1984

Cookbooks are good reading, and on a hot summer day it is fun to sit on the beach or in the shade of a tree exploring the pages and conjuring up the next winter's menus. Pages are marked and notes taken for later referrals. There are countless books which are not really cookbooks but which, for one reason or another, include discussions of food. Take for example, Kenneth Roberts' wonderful Revolutionary stories *Trending into Maine* and *Northwest Passage* which are laced with descriptions of New England food and recipes of the period. He, like my grandfather, was a writer who loved to cook, and they corresponded from time to time on this subject. Then there is Ernest Hemingway's *A Moveable Feast* and James Beard's *Delights and Prejudices* (Atheneum), both delightful to read even for non-cooks. Just the other day I found a short story written by John Steinbeck in 1983 entitled "Breakfast" and reprinted as part of a collection in *The Literary Gourmet* (Random House, 1962.); Steinbeck's enormous talent for describing a simple scene allows the aroma and taste of the eggs, bacon and biscuits to permeate the pages.

Recipes are the characters in a cookbook, some good, some bad, some simple, some not so simple and some totally outrageous. The reader must determine which the winners are. Can you taste the dish in your mind or at least have a pretty good idea of its flavor? If not, maybe it lacks enough character to whet the imagination or the ingredients are so outlandish that the taste does not present itself. When you come across a delicious character, think about how it will look finished on the plate ready to be served. In your mind's eye, picture yourself performing each step in the presentation. Do the steps seem clear and are they possible to do in your kitchen in the time you have available? Are the ingredients easily found in your supermarket? If necessary, is it possible to make substitutions without losing the character of the recipe?

Late Summer Fruits and Vegetables

Puree of vegetables can be prepared ahead and reheated just before serving. Seasoned well, they become sophisticated accompaniments. They can also be piped through large pastry tubes onto platters or plates in attractive forms.

Puree of Spinach or Broccoli

Fresh spinach—½ pound per person. Take the stems off and rinse the spinach well and cook for no more than five minutes in the water left on the leaves. Stir occasionally. It is important to drain the spinach thoroughly before putting it in a processor or blender. Add salt, pepper and a healthy sprinkle of ground mace or nutmeg. Puree and then add a drop of cream if you like. Reheat over boiling water, but not in an aluminum pot, and do not cover or the color will change.

Fresh broccoli should be washed thoroughly and broken up into small flowerets with most of the stem removed. Cook in small amounts of boiling water, adding the vegetables gradually until they are just tender. Drain well and proceed as in the recipe for spinach. A little lemon juice is a nice addition. One bunch of broccoli will feed four persons.

Applesauce

Freshly made applesauce takes no time at all to prepare and freezes well.

Ingredients:

10 Macintosh apples quartered, but not peeled or seeded

1 cup of water

¼ tablespoon of nutmeg

1 ½ tablespoons cinnamon and sugar to taste. Vanilla may also be added.

Place quartered apples in a heavy-bottomed pot and simmer the apples until soft. Drain well. Pour the remainder into a food mill over a bowl, extracting the pulp and leaving the skins and seeds behind. You will have a lovely pink applesauce that when seasoned can be served warm, at room temperature, chilled or kept in the freezer for later use. How about some gingersnaps to go with it or warm gingerbread and whipped cream?

Poached Pears with Crème Anglaise

This is a dinner party dessert for the fall that can be prepared a day or two ahead of time and looks lovely.

Ingredients:

6 pears, Bosc or Anjou, slightly under ripe

4 cups of water

2 cups of sugar

1 tablespoon fresh lemon juice

1 teaspoon grated lemon rind

1 cinnamon stick and 3 whole cloves

In a heavy pot, bring water, sugar, lemon juice and rind to a boil. Meanwhile, peel the pears, leaving the stems on, and drop immediately into cold water with a little lemon juice added to prevent discoloring. To cook, place the fruit in the boiling water along with the cinnamon stick and the cloves. Cover and keep at a rolling boil so the pears will keep moving around, until they can be pricked easily with a fork but are not mushy. Watch carefully.

When done, carefully transfer the pears with a slotted spoon to a flat-bottom dish, standing them up if possible in order to hold their shape. When they are a little cooler, the end can be trimmed so they stand up better. Pour the syrup over them and chill.

Crème Anglaise

This is a very useful sauce and complements many fruits.

Ingredients:

1 cup milk

½ cup heavy cream

1-inch piece vanilla bean

6 tablespoons sugar

4 large egg yokes

2 teaspoons cornstarch

Combine the milk, cream and vanilla bean in a saucepan and bring just to a boil. Remove from the heat and let stand ten minutes to extract the flavor of the vanilla bean. Meanwhile, beat the sugar into the egg yokes until the mixture is pale yellow and creamy, then add the cornstarch. Stir in the milk mixture, beating hard with a wire whisk. Return the mixture to a heavy saucepan and cook very slowly until the sauce is thick enough to coat the back of a silver spoon. Stir constantly with a wooden spoon all the while. This step might take fifteen minutes, but do not let the sauce boil or it might curdle from the heat. Let cool, stirring often, and remove the vanilla bean. Cover with plastic wrap and refrigerate.

To serve:

Spoon some sauce over the bottom of each dessert plate and place a pear in the center of each or stand the pears up on a round serving platter after pouring some sauce in the bottom. Pass the rest of the Crème Anglaise separately.

Library Dining

Libraries are a luxury not always found in newer apartments or houses, but if you have a dining area, or alcove, it can become a combination library and dining room. There is something cozy about eating in a library. It can be done as simply or lavishly as you want. Both sides of a dining alcove can be lined with bookshelves, with a round table and a long cloth and couple of chairs added for everyday use. A long table can also double as a desk-and-dinner table. One wall can be a mirror reflecting the books onto the other wall, with a single banquette holding lots of pillows set against it and a table that can be pulled up for dining. The point of this discussion is this: if dining areas or other rooms are not used frequently, think of setting a party table there. I have a friend in Paris who has much more taste than money, but who likes to give seated dinners for eight. Her living room is too small for everyone to sit for cocktails as well as hold the dinner table. She has solved the problem by setting up the table in her bedroom where she has arranged the furniture to leave room for the table. So when she has a dinner, she in fact has a dining room.

Tips

Use a plant sprayer to spray bread with water twice during baking for a crustier loaf.

Rub chicken with vegetable oil before placing into bags for freezing.

Quote

"At a dinner party
One should eat wisely
But not to well,
And talk well
But not too wisely."
—W. Somerset Maugham

Letter # 9

THANKSGIVING, 1984

In the early seventies, shortly before the revolution there, I was in Lisbon, Portugal, which was busy building new offices and hotels to bring that old city into the twentieth century. At midday, everything stops for three hours and the main meal of the day is taken. It was hot walking up the steep streets, and I was looking forward to the coolness that envelopes one upon entering a restaurant in a stone building—as it is much softer than air conditioning. My thoughts were diverted by the sight of two workmen having their lunch in a shady spot on a construction site close to a noisy intersection. They had mentally wiped out their surroundings and had set a table for lunch. The table was an upside-down crate which had been covered with a starchy white cloth and two napkins. Two glass tumblers, a bottle of red wine and a loaf of the wonderful coarse Portuguese bread had been placed on the cloth in readiness for the main dish, which was warming in a metal container over a one-burner stove nearby. These two Portuguese men in their traditional dark blue work clothes were lunching with as much style as the bankers at their club down the street. For them, their environment and pocketbook had nothing to do with the manner in which they were accustomed to eat.

Pumpkin Pie

Ingredients:

Pâté brisée to fit a 9-inch pie plate with the addition of one teaspoon sugar (recipe below)

¾ cup sugar

1 teaspoon each of ginger and cinnamon

¼ teaspoon each of salt, ground cloves and nutmeg

2 cups of pumpkin puree

2 tablespoons of dark unsulfured molasses

3 eggs

1 ½ cups light cream

2 tablespoons brandy

Preheat oven to 375°F.

In a bowl or food processor blend together the sugar, spices, pumpkin puree and molasses. Either mix the remaining ingredients in another bowl and then add to the pumpkin mixture or gradually add them through the top of your processor. Pour the mixture into the prepared pie shell, either bought or homemade, and bake in a 375°F oven thirty-five to forty minutes. Cool and freeze. Reheat in a slow oven after thawing. Serve with sweetened whipped cream, vanilla or pecan ice cream.

Pâté Brisée (For Two Crusts)

Ingredients:

3 ½ cups flour

2 teaspoons salt

2 ½ sticks frozen chopped sweet butter

4 tablespoons shortening (such as Crisco or lard)

⅔ to 1 cup ice water

Combine all ingredients quickly in a food processor, turning motor on and off, just enough for the ingredients to hold together. You should see little pieces of butter. Wrap in plastic wrap and refrigerate two hours or until firm. On a floured surface, using a rolling pin dusted with flour, roll dough out into a thin circle larger than your pie plate, brush the flour off the dough, roll up on the rolling pin and unroll onto the pie plate. Make a high fluted edge with your fingers after fitting the dough into the plate. Prick the bottom with a fork several times and refrigerate for one hour or freeze for later use. Line the shell with wax paper, fill the paper with rice and bake in a 400°F oven for ten minutes. Carefully remove the rice and paper and bake for another ten to fifteen minutes until the shell is light colored. Now it is ready for the filling.

The following is a light and easy cocktail accompaniment.

Cream Cheese Canapes

Ingredients:

1 large package softened cream cheese or Farmers cheese

¼ cup finely chopped chives

½ cup finely chopped celery

Salt and pepper

1 large bunch parsley finely chopped

Toothpicks

In a bowl mix the cheese, celery, salt and pepper to taste with your hands. Form into small balls and roll in the chopped parsley. Insert a toothpick in each one and refrigerate until balls are firm. They look very pretty on a silver plate.

A Little Lafite for Tomorrow Night

It is almost impossible to imagine, but what if at the end of a dinner party you found yourself with a half empty (or half full, depending upon your frame of mind) bottle of wine? What should you do? Drink it now? No, it is too late. Put it in tomorrow's casserole? Shocking! No, there is an answer to your dilemma. Keep a couple of half-decanters or bottles on hand for just such an unusual emergency and decant the leftover (I hate to use the word leftover with your Lafite) wine into it and then pump the bottle if possible. It is the excess of air that quickly affects the wine, especially the whites, so if there is less air in the bottle it keeps a bit longer. A full half of white will keep a couple of days and red will last for up to a week. It is even a better idea to have a little dinner ádeux . . . you, your friend and your little leftover Lafite the next night.

Quote

"The only real elegance is in the mind; if you've got that, the rest really comes from it."

—Diana Vreeland

Letter # 10

CHRISTMAS, 1984

Christmas cheer, my dear friends, can be elusive until the last store has closed on the last shopper and there is no solution for what has not been done or given or sent. Christmas Eve is the best and loveliest part of Christmas because what has been wrapped and given has not yet been opened and what has been bought and prepared has not yet been eaten. Good food and wine returns one's sense of humor, and even the children seem better in candlelight. How to arrive at this moment of joy and good cheer is the trick. A simply elegant dinner, the phrase to be taken literally here, is called for to compliment this great holy night. This is the night for caviar; price the West Coast variety as it is very good and much more affordable than the imported. A little goes a long way if you spread it on the toast rounds ahead and decorate them with finely chopped onions and grated egg yolk. To keep the children out of the caviar serve them toast rounds spread with the best peanut butter and sprinkled with finely crumbled crisp bacon. Beef is so easy, if it is not on the menu for Christmas day: filet mignon for a small group, a whole filet or rib roast for a larger number. Potatoes or rice can be prepared well ahead and so can a vegetable. For dessert order a búche de Noel at the pastry shop, try the mocha, and for heaven's sake sit down and relax; you will have produced a "Simply Elegant Dinner."

Tournedos Moreteur

Ingredients:

8 slices beef tenderloin ¾ to 1 inch thick

8 slices of French bread sautéed in butter

2 shallots chopped

1 cup white wine

2 tablespoons anchovy butter (2 teaspoons of butter mixed with 2 teaspoons anchovy paste).

In a heavy skillet brown the filets, straight from the refrigerator, in very hot butter for about three minutes on each side for rare. Place each filet on a round of French bread and keep warm. If the butter in the pan is too burned pour it out and heat new butter. Add shallots, stir for a minute and then add the anchovy butter. Then add the wine and cook down for two or three minutes. Pour over the tournedos and serve at once.

This is an easy recipe and goes quickly if all the ingredients have been measured ahead and stored in custard cups or other small dishes, then covered with a plastic wrap.

Roast Beef

Order a well-aged rib roast, the first cut, as many ribs as you require. Do not have it boned but have the chine or backbone removed and then tied back on again. Rub the meat well with one tablespoon salt, one teaspoon freshly ground pepper and two teaspoons of crumbled rosemary. Preheat the oven for at least fifteen minutes at 500°F. Place the meat on a rack in a shallow roasting pan and place it in the oven. Roast for twenty minutes and then turn the heat down to 350°F and continue roasting for about another hour. A meat thermometer is essential. Cook to 130°F for very rare, 140°F for medium rare. Remember that the roast will continue to cook even after it is removed from the oven. Let it rest for at least fifteen minutes before carving.

Le Beau Cochon

I will never forget the Christmas my mother brought a roast suckling pig to the table. My sister and I looked aghast at the crispy, curly-tailed whole animal lying there on the table with a mouth full of a shiny red apple, while penetrating us with beady eyes which even had eye lashes. Well, we ran from the table in tears leaving the adults systematically dissecting the pig. When I grew up I did the same thing to my children with the same results. Roasting a pig is simple and is the most delicious thing to eat. It is awesome on a buffet table! This recipe is followed annually and is from James Beard's *American Cookery* (Little Brown and Company).

Roast Suckling Pig

Ingredients:

1 large (approximately 12 pounds), or two smaller fresh pigs, depending on the size of your pans, oven and number of guests.

1 orange

2 lemons

2 bay leaves

2 sprigs rosemary

Oil, olive or peanut

4 large bunches parsley

Butter and cream

Celery stalk with some green on it, or a sprig of berried holly

Rub the pig with lemon and stuff the cavity with two bay leaves, a generous slice of orange zest, a sprig of rosemary and a bunch of parsley. Sew up the cavity. Place him on his knees in a roasting pan. The snout will probably protrude beyond the edge, so wrap foil around it to take the drippings. Put little balls of foil in the eye sockets and cover the ears with foil. Rub him with oil. This can be done ahead of time and he can then wait in any cool place until you are ready to roast him. A 12-pound pig will take two and a half hours at 350°F and the smaller ones about two hours. The first half hour baste him a couple of times with a mixture of 1 part melted butter to 2 parts cream and one hour later baste again with just melted butter. One hour later baste with a mixture of melted butter and the pan juices. At the end of the cooking remove the pig to a large platter and let rest at least fifteen or twenty minutes before carving.

Take a knife, or better yet a pair of kitchen scissors and slit the skin down the length on either side of the backbone and down the shoulders. Now take a sharp knife and separate the meat and skin from the ribs working from top to bottom.

Presenting the Pig

Surround the pig on the platter with masses of parsley leaves, place a wreath of greens around his neck (ivy is very easy and looks pretty) and put the stalk of celery or sprig of holly in his mouth. For a cocktail party or buffet dinner, let him be admired for a while and then carve him right there and serve on small warm tortillas with shredded green onions for garnish. What a way to go! By the way, don't forget to remove the foil from his eyes.

It is perfectly possible to roast the pig outside in a pan on your grill with the top down.

Aged Eggnog

Remember that when you make eggnog all the ingredients must be first class, your liquors the best and use extra large fresh eggs. The recipe calls for half and half and I changed it to milk and cream, but you have your choice.

Ingredients:

2 cups cognac

1 cup Jamaican rum

½ cup of a very smooth bourbon whisky

½ cup medium dry sherry

12 eggs

¾ cup sugar

2 quarts either half and half or 1 quart very fresh milk and

1 quart very fresh cream (not whipping)

Mix the brandy, rum, whisky and sherry and set aside. Separate the eggs in two large bowls and proceed to beat the egg yokes with a whisk until just blended and then beat in the sugar. Slowly add first the liquor and then the milk and cream or half and half. Beat the egg whites until they stand in peaks and carefully fold into the yoke mixture. Cover and let age in the refrigerator for at least two or three days before serving. When serving, sprinkle some thinly julienned lemon zest on top of the eggnog. So now you can enjoy an almost totally do-it-yourself Christmas and be of good cheer at the same time.

From the *Oxford Book of Carols*

Because the Christmas carol was derived from dance music, it did not arrive until well after the puritanical middle ages and well into the medieval period. It was a creation of the fifteenth century, an expression of the release from the suppression of dance and theatre during the proceeding centuries.

> "All out of darkness we have light,
> Which made the angels sing this night
> Glory to God and peace to men
> Now and forever more, Amen

Letter # 11

NEW YEAR, 1985

Christmas, as you know, is not just one great meal perfectly planned and executed but most often an endless assortment of meals before and after. Whatever the case may be, "leftovers" is certainly not a very appealing word to apply to the menu for a day or two after the celebration. Therefore, good dishes deserve more poetic names. For example, creamed turkey or chicken should become "Chicken Tetrazzini" with a few easy additions and cold roast beef can end up as "Sautéed au Poivre"

Chicken Tetrazzini Plus

Ingredients:

Julienned cooked turkey or chicken

Sautéed sliced mushrooms

A light cream sauce with a little sherry added

Salt, pepper and nutmeg to taste

Cooked spaghetti or green linguini

Parmesan cheese, grated

Mix all the ingredients together and spread in a buttered gratin dish. Sprinkle with more cheese and bake at 350°F until lightly browned.

Roast Beef au Poivre

Ingredients:

4 thick slices of rare roast beef (the rarest)

2 tablespoons cracked pepper

¼ pound of butter

½ cup sifted flour

4 tablespoons olive oil

¼ cup cognac

½ cup beef stock, fresh or bought

2 teaspoons lemon juice

1 tablespoon of minced parsley or chives

Salt both sides of the beef slices and then press the cracked pepper into the meat with the heel of your hand. Cream the butter until soft and smooth and spread half of it on both sides of the beef slices to hold the pepper. Refrigerate, wrapped in wax paper, for one hour or more. Measure the remaining ingredients. Heat the oil in a heavy skillet until smoking hot. Dip the slices in the flour, shaking off the excess and sauté a couple of minutes on each side, just to heat through and become crusty. Store on a platter in a warm oven. Pour off most of the fat, lower the heat somewhat, add the cognac and let it cook almost away. Then add the stock, raise the heat and reduce by half. Take off the heat and add the parsley, lemon juice and remaining butter. Stir until smooth and pour over the beef slices.

From Michael Field's *Culinary Classics and Improvisations* (Alfred A. Knopf).

"Where's the Beef"

A note in a recent financial newsletter tells us that for the first time consumption of poultry has surpassed beef in the United States. Seeing the handwriting on the wall, my husband sold off his herd of beef cattle (each original cow was named for an old girlfriend but he has never said who the bulls were named for). The rancher who took care of them in Mississippi also saw the handwriting on the wall and he created a large pond in one of his pastures and is now busily raising catfish. It is possible to raise two thousand pounds per acre of some strains. Catfish can grow from fingerlings to twenty pounds in about six months and some can mature at one hundred and twenty pounds. They are rather homely fish, but then so are sturgeons, and look what they produce. The rancher feeds his fish Purina Dog Chow which he dispenses by simply driving around his pond in a grain harvesting machine raining pellets over the frantically rising fish. A pioneer catfish raiser in Tennessee has found that these fish, when raised in the higher elevations in clear swift streams, produce an excellent roe which he plans to market. So forget about the swimming pool; build a pond instead and produce caviar.

How To Cook Your Goose (Stuffed Goose Foster)

The following is a family recipe for stuffing and cooking a pair of Canada Geese.

Ingredients:

2 oven-ready Canada or farm-raised geese at room temperature

1 bag seasoned poultry stuffing soaked in milk in a large bowl until soft

⅔ of a large green pepper

1 cup chopped onion, but not too fine

⅔ cup chopped celery tops packed tight

1 can garbanzo beans

3 eggs

Salt and pepper

Chop the pepper, onions and celery by hand or in a processor and sauté slowly in butter for twenty minutes. Drain and rinse beans, discarding any loose skins and, in a large bowl, add to bread stuffing. Let onion mix cool and add to the stuffing mix. Beat 3 eggs with a fork and pour over stuffing mix. Add seasonings and mix with your hands. Put aside. Wash and dry birds and rub the outside with celery salt, garlic salt and thyme. Stuff the birds and place in a roasting pan covered. Cut bacon strips in half and lay across the breast. A little crushed foil in the vent will hold in the stuffing. Add 1 cup of water to the pan, a couple stalks of celery, and one small sliced orange. Cover and bake in a 300°F oven until fork tender. Remove the cover and raise temperature to 350°F for crisping. Let the bird rest on a platter for a few minutes before carving.

The Party's Over

Without going into all the boring details of the consequences of December's merrymaking, there are some easy ways to get back on track and off the scale in January. In Craig Claiborne's *Gourmet Diet* (Time Books), there is a very informative introduction by Jane Brody. She accurately says that many people are under the misconception that carbohydrates, the white foods I call them, such as rice, potatoes, spaghetti, kidney beans and bread, are more fattening than proteins. That is not the case, as there is often a higher fat content in protein food; witness the examples below. Jane Brody uses the dieter's favorite, 5 ounces lean steak, for her comparisons.

1 five-ounce steak (that is small!) = 500 calories

1 medium potato (plain) = 131 calories

5 ounces cooked rice = 154 calories

5 ounces spaghetti = 157 calories

5 ounces kidney beans = 167 calories

5 ounces bread = 390 calories

If you simply substitute ounce for ounce carbohydrates for fat, you will automatically cut back on your calories without giving up the pleasure of eating. Add to your menu vegetables, salads, and fresh fruits which contribute the necessary vitamins, minerals and roughage (caloric fiber).

Brody's introduction states that the sweet tasting fruits are much more satisfying than manufactured sweets.

How to apply this knowledge to daily menus is easy. But I am sure that you have read a thousand diets published in books and magazines. They are absolutely crazy. It would be necessary to shop every day in order to conform to their exotic regimes. Few daily menus have repeat ingredients—if you are allowed to have half of something on Monday, the other half usually doesn't appear in a later meal. They are impossible diets if you are required to eat out often or if you have to prepare other meals for non-dieters in the family. In fact, they are totally impractical and therefore difficult to maintain. The simpler the rules the easier it is to lose weight gracefully, and without telling everyone else at the table that you are dieting, a real no-no.

Stay away from red meat as much as possible—at a dinner party eat half a portion.

Carbohydrates induce relaxation, so are perfect evening foods.

Breakfast is an important meal, so do not skip it. Eat dark breads and use low fat yogurt and salt-free cereal. On the days you have an egg, don't eat meat. Have as many meatless days as possible.

Seafood is excellent any time.

Menu to Lose By

Two ounces of stir-fried meat will go a long way when combined with stir-fried vegetables and a bowl of rice. Cooked pasta mixes with a little grated cheese, or any meatless sauce, white clam sauce, peas and mushrooms, or smoked salmon.

Bean salads with onions and peppers.

Filet of fish brushed on both sides with mayonnaise and broiled and seasoned with fresh dill and lime.

Raw clams and oysters or sushi.

Baked potato with caviar, with fresh ground black pepper or with low fat yogurt and freshly ground black pepper.

Soups thickened with potatoes, and bean soups.

Minestrone is delicious with black bread, a little goat cheese and fruit.

What Is a Reasonable Drink?

1 ½ ounces of 80-proof liquor

1-ounce of 110-proof

2 twelve-ounce glasses of beer

2 five-ounce glasses of French wine

2 four-ounce glasses of American wine (more alcohol)

The equivalent of one cocktail and two glasses of wine are generally thought to be a reasonable daily amount.

Chinese Cooking

I recently received a book entitled *Pat Tung's Cooking School. A Complete Course in Chinese Cuisine,* (Simon and Schuster Inc.). Pat Hsu Tung was born in Shanghai, has lived in Taiwan, now lives in Ohio and has been running her own cooking school for some time.

The progression of instructions is very easy to follow. She has tried to cut down the preparation time, so as not to discourage the cook, and pays great attention to limiting ingredients that are considered nutritionally poor. All this is accomplished without losing the great beauty and taste of Chinese cuisine. Starting with this issue, and for the next couple of months, I will be relaying to you some of the very helpful information from this cookbook and hope it will encourage you to experiment in a different culinary medium and to buy this wonderfully simple guide to "China a Table." My husband who lived for three years behind the lines in China during the war will follow with his suggestions of what to drink with a Chinese meal.

First off, let's define the four regions of Chinese cuisine.

The first is **Mandarin** or **Peking** from the north. This is the breadbasket of China so there are lots of dumplings, noodles and pancakes. Here also is the home of the famous Peking duck. Pat Tung says that the cooking of this province is simple, with few dishes stir-fried and that there is a liberal use of garlic, green onions, ginger root, star anise and peppercorns. Wine is also used in the cooking here.

Shanghai—the eastern seacoast. Here is the richest soil in China, with a long growing season, with two crops of rice a year and an abundance of seafood, vegetables and livestock. Pat Tung describes the cuisine as rich and elaborate. More oil is used in cooking, and sugar arrives as a flavor. The simple dumplings of the north become delicate, tiny meat-filled rolls, not to forget spring rolls and wontons. This region is the home of Red-cooking.

Cantonese—Southeast coast. Now we have moved to a sub-tropical place where seafood and produce are again very available, but there is less use of soy sauce and more of oyster sauce and fermented black beans. Eye appeal is important here, especially color. This is light, delicate food with many sauces. You will find the tomato here, a holdover from the great early trading era with the western cultures. I would have to say that dim sum is one of my favorite foods here but also one recognizes many other familiar names such as chow mein, meaning literally stir-fried noodles.

Szechuan and Hunan—This region is inland and is in the south central part of the country. This is the land of hot and spicy dishes with chili peppers used in every way possible. Again, much use of garlic, ginger root and green onions. Tartness, sweetness, pungency and fragrance are the characteristics of this cooking.

Here is a sample of simple main dishes served with rice.

Red Cooked Shrimp in the Shell

Ingredients (serves 4):

1 pound large fresh shrimp in the shell (I shell the shrimp for easier eating)

2 green onions

2 slivers ginger root

3 cloves garlic

2 tablespoons oil (peanut or corn)

1 tablespoon sherry

1 tablespoon soy sauce

2 teaspoons sugar

1 teaspoon hoisin sauce

With a sharp knife or scissors cut up the back of the shrimp enough to devein. Wash and dry with toweling.

Chop green onions into ⅛-inch pieces. Pare ginger and crush the garlic.

Heat the oil on high in a Wok. The electric ones are well worth buying. Add the ginger and the garlic and remove them when they turn brown. Add the shrimp and turn over when they turn pink. Add all the other ingredients and stir-fry for about two minutes. Turn off the heat and add the scallions. Stir and serve immediately with a bowl or rice. If you like, add some fresh oil to the Wok and quickly stir-fry some fresh snow peas for a vegetable.

Plain Rice

The Chinese judge the ratio of rice to cooking water by the hand, not the cup. Place your hand flat over the rice in the pot and add water until it comes 3 quarters of the way up your hand. The ratio is correct. However, the following is a measured recipe for the precise cook.

Ingredients (serves 4):

1 cup long grain rice

1 ¾ cups cold water

Measure the rice and rinse it, raking it with your hands until the water runs clear through the rice. In China this is a ritual that signifies the beginning of the preparation of the meal. Add the cold water and bring to a boil over medium heat and let it bubble for just one minute. Turn the heat to the lowest, cover, and let the rice simmer for twenty minutes, not a minute longer. You must adjust the time according to how hot "low" is on your stove. Do not take the top off to look while it is steaming. When you turn the heat off leave the pot covered for five minutes. Rice will keep this way for up to thirty minutes if the top is not disturbed. Just fluff it with a fork at serving time. It does not have to be very warm. Rice comes with a Chinese meal in individual bowls so that the diner can add sauces, meat, fish etc. to his or her bowl of rice, stirring it in and eating with the bowl held close to the mouth in one hand and the chopsticks in the other.

Tips from Thibaut: What Do You Drink with Chinese Food

A few years ago the Tastevins, devotees of Burgundian wine, planned a Chinese banquet as a wine tasting event. Despite having E.M. Pei, the great architect and food connoisseur, in charge of the dinner, the tasting was a total disaster: the spices, which made the food so good, destroyed the taste of the wines. Lesson: don't try to mix fine wines with Chinese foods. If you must have a wine to accompany a Chinese meal, have a Portuguese rosé which is heavy enough to withstand the effects of the spices or try a sweet sauterne from the Bordeaux with the soup, which usually ends a great Chinese meal. As for me, I order Chinese Tsintao beer. The Chinese sauces, particularly soy, give great thirst and beer is a good thirst quencher.

—Thibaut de Saint Phalle

"*Home-Making*" is the biggest job in the world; it bosses them all. It hangs over the others like a storm cloud, or a ray of sunlight, as the case may be. It is the gigantic hub of the wheel of life, with its radiating spokes of lesser positions on which the world rides to its destiny . . .

"Hidden beneath the exterior of every personality there is a spark of idealism—of ambition. Most every woman in the world has a secret longing to better her own condition and to help to make the world "homelike."

—Ida C. Bailey Allen,
"Mrs. Allen on Cooling, Menu, Service"
(Doubleday, Page and Company, 1924)

Letter # 12

WINTER 1985

Washington D.C. conducts its business and general information gathering (gossip) across the catered table in every rentable, borrowable place in town. About seventy-five percent of caterers' clients are corporate and the rest are charitable or private. The catering business is very old, very large and highly competitive.

Entertaining in Washington is, and always has been, dictated by the "Capital Calendar." Traditionally, due to the heat in July and August, the Congress disappears and, even with the introduction of air conditioning, the town is empty during these months. The season runs from late September until the Fourth of July recess excepting three weeks or so at Christmas and Easter. The early legislators did not often bring their families to Washington with them, partly due to the lack of safe comfortable travel and the cost of maintaining two households. Representing one's state or district in Washington did not start out as a full-time vocation but as a service rendered to the country for several periods during the year. Bread and butter money was earned back home on the farm, the ranch, in trade, the law, etc. and wives were more often than not left at home as overseers of the family enterprises. Congressional sessions were shorter, geared toward planting or harvest times. Legislators, therefore, tended to live in rooming houses or small hotels up near the Capital.

Entertaining was done either at clubs or in hotels and so these establishments were forced to turn to outside help in the busy season. Here was the acorn from which the catering oak grew. Here too, the cocktail buffet was invented. These parties were simply an extension of the legislative day with the pleasant addition of food and drink. It also avoided the problem of running a seated dinner without a hostess.

Cocktail receptions are alive and well; as one senatorial staffer put it to me, "I have yet to buy my own dinner in Washington, I simply fill up at one of the reception buffets to which my staff is invited each day." No delicate little tidbits at these parties; there are buckets of shrimps and oysters, roast beefs and hams and tables of sweets with smiling corporate heads and their lobbyists to greet the guests. And they arrive like a swarm of locusts descending on the "fatted calf," shaking a few hands, giving and taking a few rumors and then heading off to the next "reception." Even the arrival of beautiful women hardly causes a comma in a conversation unless of course her name is a Power or Next-to-Power name. Power is always the most popular guest at the party, the greatest aphrodisiac in town, fickle, flirtatious and evasive.

Capital entertaining is influenced by current events. From the end of the war until the sixties foreign embassies competed furiously with each other for official Washington's attention. Everyone wanted to do business with the United States or receive manna from Congress. Ambassador Zahedi of Iran probably took the party prize with his endless punch bowls of caviar and his seated dinners at which the tables were set entirely with gold cutlery, plates and gold-rimmed crystal, all bearing the crown of the Shah.

What's in a Name?

Even though the name seems exotic, a squab is nothing more than a four week old pigeon. They are, however, not tough like pigeons but instead have tender, sweet dark meat. They are at their best when the limbs are eaten with the fingers, so think twice about adding a sauce.

Simply stuff one to a person with seasoned wild or brown rice and sage, and set them in a shallow roasting pan. Sprinkle them with salt and pepper, pour on a little brandy and let them set for at least an hour. For six birds add ¼ cup port or Madeira and roast in a hot 450°F oven for thirty-five minutes. Baste twice with juices in the pan. What is most important is not to over-cook the birds, so set a timer. Lay them cartwheel style on a round platter or directly on the plates, and in the center place a hollowed out orange filled with currant or jelly for each bird. Garnish the platter or plates with watercress.

Grape Stuffing for Squabs

Ingredients:

4 dozen Muscat grapes peeled and seeded

½ cup fine bread crumbs

Salt and pepper

1 tablespoon brandy

Stuff 6 birds and continue as above

Pigeonneaux á la Normande

In an ovenproof casserole dish on top of the stove melt 4 tablespoons of butter and brown 6 trussed squabs. Season with salt and pepper, cover and roast in the oven for thirty minutes at 350°F. Spread a layer of warm, slightly sweetened applesauce on a platter and settle the birds on top. Pour 2 tablespoons of warm heavy cream over each squab and serve immediately.

These recipes can be used for small Rock Cornish game hens, but they will need at least ten minutes more cooking time. There is no comparison between the fresh and frozen game hen, but until recently the fresh were almost impossible to find. The frozen are apt to be dry and stringy when cooked.

Squabs are a favorite dinner party choice since they can be prepared for the oven ahead of time and put in to roast a half hour before you sit down. Wild rice compliments the grape stuffing, and a bright winter vegetable such as Brussels sprouts with chestnuts, goes well with the rice stuffed birds.

Brussels Sprouts with Chestnuts

Cook Brussels sprouts until tender, dropping them into boiling salted water one at a time so the water temperature does not drop. This preserves the greenness. When a small knife penetrates the sprouts easily, drain them and combine with chestnuts and melted butter. You can purchase shelled chestnuts in jars or tins and simply add warm to the vegetable. You might want to halve them first.

Fantastic Chicken

Ingredients (serves 2, or twenty appetizers):

2 boned chicken breasts

Marinade:

1 teaspoon sherry

½ teaspoon cornstarch

½ teaspoon salt

⅛ teaspoon black pepper

1 egg beaten

Coating:

½ cup cornstarch

½ cup sesame seeds

½ cup sliced almonds

1 egg beaten

1 cup or more of peanut oil for frying

Wash and dry the chicken and pound gently between sheets of wax paper. Cut each halve into 10 or 12 pieces for appetizers or leave them whole as a main course. Place the chicken in the marinade for twenty minutes. Measure the cornstarch on one plate and the sesame seeds and almonds on the other. Beat the egg in a bowl. Dip the chicken first in the cornstarch then in the egg and finally in the almonds. You can prepare the chicken up to this point and refrigerate it until later. Fry the pieces for four or five minutes in the oil after which they are removed and drained. Serve with hot mustard or sweet and sour sauce.

Stir-Fried Asparagus

Ingredients:

1 pound asparagus (thin)

3 tablespoons oil

¼ teaspoon salt

1 teaspoon oyster sauce

Cut the tough ends off the asparagus and rinse them in cold water. Slice the stalks diagonally into 2-inch pieces and store in a bowl of cold water if they must wait. When you are ready to stir-fry, remove and dry the asparagus and stir-fry in hot oil for about ten turns. Add the oyster sauce and salt and continue cooking until the vegetable takes on a nice green color.

Consommé Bellevue

A dinner party soup from the Victorian era in Newport.

Mix 3 cups of good, clear beef or chicken broth with 3 cups of clear clam broth and heat to the boiling point. Divide into heated bowls and top with a soup spoon of unsweetened whipped cream.

Variations: Put the bowls under the broiler for a minute to glaze the whipped cream.

Inauguration Dinner

"As the fifteenth President got into his carriage and drove away, the sixteenth waved to him until he was gone. Then Lincoln went into the house.

Dinner was a haphazard affair. Seventeen sat down for dinner in the so called family dining room on the ground floor. Miss Lane's taste was for plain cooking, which suited Lincoln but not Mary or the ladies, who had dreamed of lobsters and canvasback duck and soft shelled crabs and Potomac shad with roe instead of sturdy roast beef."

—Gore Vidal, *Lincoln* (Random House)

Letter # 13

LATE WINTER 1985

Eggs

Egg dishes can be appetizing at any time of day or any time of year. Important, though, is to select the large brown organic eggs which will provide you with beautiful deep yellow yolks and firm shells. Look at the box to see where the eggs come from, hopefully a local source, for freshness. The importance of freshness is well illustrated by the soufflé, as ones made with old or small eggs never rise as well. Following are some suggestions for cooking eggs.

Poached Eggs

Consider poaching eggs in stock, soup, wine, or herb flavored liquids.

Crisp, unbuttered toast with the crust removed is a perfect bed for a poached egg. When poaching eggs in plain water add 2 tablespoons more or less of white vinegar to the cooking water to help hold the egg whites together. First bring the water to a boil and then lower to just a simmer. Now drop in the eggs and immediately push the egg whites back over the yokes with a slotted spoon moving the egg gently to avoid sticking. Simmer the egg for three minutes then remove with a slotted spoon. Drain well and pat dry, if necessary. They can be trimmed to perfect rounds with a knife or kitchen scissors and can also be held for later use in a bowl of cold water.

Never-Fail Eggs Benedict

Place a slice of ham on top of a toasted, buttered English muffin half and then sit a soft poached egg on the top. The yolk must be runny to mix with the hollandaise sauce. Cover with hollandaise sauce and sprinkle with paprika or simply place a thin slice of truffle on top. Serve at once.

Although the traditional dish does not call for tomato, if ripe ones are available a slice on top of the ham is delicious. For variety, try different types of ham or even a slice of smoked salmon and experiment with different varieties of toasted bread.

Hollandaise Sauce

Place 4 eggs, 2 tablespoons of real lemon juice and a pinch of cayenne in a blender. Cover the container and run the motor on low speed until well blended and then remove the cover and add bubbling hot, not browned, melted sweet butter in a slow steady stream. Salted butter burns at a much lower temperature. When all the butter has been added, turn off the machine and you have hollandaise ready to serve. To reheat place over, *not in*, hot, *not boiling*, water and heat, stirring, until warm. This is not a sauce to be served hot. Hollandaise sauce can be frozen, as long as it is defrosted on the counter before warming.

Scrambled Eggs

In a bowl beat the required number of eggs (2 per person) with either a fork or wire whisk and some salt and pepper until no lumps of either whites or yokes are seen. The salt will help break up the lumps. Do not add any liquid to the eggs at this time as they will only end up runny. Slowly heat a little butter (preferably sweet) in a frying pan until just melted. Have the lowest possible heat when adding the eggs and stir gently but continually just until there are no translucent pieces of white. The eggs should never fry. If you like, a little whipping cream can then be added (1 tablespoon per serving). Other ingredients could be added at this point also but herbs would be added to the mixing bowl; chopped fresh dill is a favorite. To cut down on the cholesterol content: for two people use 2 egg yokes and 4 egg whites.

Superior Scrambled Eggs

Using a double boiler, a bowl placed over a pot of simmering water or a chafing dish is an ideal way to scramble eggs because a constant low temperature is easy to maintain. Stir constantly with a wooden spoon which assures smoothness and delicacy and lowers the chance of overcooking. Don't forget that eggs continue to cook even after they have been removed from the heat, therefore, remove them from the heat a little early.

Hard-Cooked Eggs

Here is the one time that really fresh eggs are not desirable as they will be impossible to peel. Older eggs have developed a little space between the egg and the shell which makes the peeling possible.

Cook the eggs in simmering water for ten minutes and then immediately plunge them into a bowl of cold water. This prevents a dark ring from forming around the yoke and allows moisture to condense between the egg and the shell, separating the two, and allowing for easy peeling. You can peel the eggs as soon as they are cool enough to handle. When you want stuffed eggs for hors-d'oeuvre, buy the smallest ones to be found as they are much easier to eat.

Settings

There is a book titled *The Perfect Setting* authored by Peri Wolfman and Charles Gold. The publisher is Harry N. Abrams Inc. In many cases, they have gone into someone's home to create and photograph table settings using items belonging to the owner. It is a book filled with ideas for every taste and pocketbook, some arrangements costing no more than the time it takes to place them on the table. For example, they make frequent use of lovely paper lace doilies as place mats accompanied by linen napkins often laced trimmed. Used in gold they look very chic. In one photograph they sit on a pine table in front of a centerpiece of green apples, bosc pears and bunches of asparagus tied with the glittery gold ribbon you find at Christmas. Green ivy was used as filler and the feeling is of soft greens and golds. An amusing table is the one set for a Chinese take-out dinner. Bamboo trays are the place mats and blue and white checkered kitchen towels are the napkins. Each tray is fitted out with a napkin, chopsticks, a chopstick rest, a Chinese export carp-design rice bowl and a little white teapot to use with a small tea cup without a handle.

There are also individual ramekins for the hot mustard sauce. Any of these items can be purchased at minimal cost from export shops such as Pier 1. The Chinese take-out containers are opened and fitted neatly into two willow boxes and set in the center of the table. A nice touch was the extra take-out container used to fill with simple bouquet of flowers. At the back of the book is a source section of catalogues and stores across the country that specialize in linen, glasses, flatware etc. It would be a fine gift for a bride but buy one for yourself too.

Yogurt Cheese

Yogurt cheese is made with either regular or low fat yogurt. Simply spoon some yogurt into a very fine sieve or a colander lined with cheese cloth, or even use a coffee filter and placed over a bowl. Cover and refrigerate for the night which allows time for the whey to ooze through into the bowl. Serve it plain or with some herbs de Provence sprinkled on top. It makes a great dieter's cheese.

Fromage de Chevré Mariné á l' Huile d'Herbes

Ingredients (serves 6):

6 small goat cheeses (Picodon, Crottin, or Cabecou)

½ clove garlic peeled

¼ teaspoon each dried rosemary and thyme

1 bay leaf

6 whole black peppercorns

6 whole white peppercorns

6 whole coriander seeds

1 cup good olive oil

Cut each cheese in half horizontally and place in a wide-mouthed half-pint jar. Put in the herbs and spices and cover with oil. Close tightly and store in a cool place, not the refrigerator, for at least a week.

To serve, remove the cheese from the jar, straining the oil back into the jar. Broil the cheese until just warm and serve with slices of warm French bread. This recipe is the traditional way of storing the firmer goat cheeses and extending their life.

Mouthwatering! Use the cheese within a month. The above recipe comes from Lillo, a cheese shop that is worth visiting at 35 Rue des Belles-Feuilles, near the Place Victor-Hugo in Paris.

Tips from Thibaut:
From Your Roving Correspondent

If you want to have an unusual and enjoyable visit abroad, try Copenhagen. For centuries the Danes have wandered about seeking conquest and creating turmoil. They conquered Britain, pillaged the continent and even discovered North America. Today they have learned that they have enough islands in their own homeland to find adventure whenever they need it. Although Danes, Swedes and Norwegians all understand each other's language, they are very different. At S.A.S. they say the Danes furnish the pilot, the Norwegians those lovely blond stewardesses and the Swedes the management and the money.

Denmark is a country where life is to be enjoyed. I am particularly fond of Danish food. It is no wonder. It is an agricultural country and the fish is usually good. If you want a special meal, try a small chic restaurant near the waterfront, two blocks from the royal palace called Els (the Elk). You might start with a venison paté with loganberries, followed by perhaps the best turbot you have ever tasted. It is not smothered with hollandaise but gently braised and served in its own juices along with very fresh greens cooked as the French do—just enough to be tender and yet retain their flavor. After you have explored Copenhagen, try the out-islands by ferry, unless of course, you are a sailor. Then bare boat charter your way to the islands in the summer months. Bring a friend or a companion and enjoy a northern odyssey. The Danes are very special people and smile often. This is what makes foreign visits enjoyable.

—Thibaut de Saint Phalle

In Paris, the Grand Vefour is serving champagne by the carafe. Not Taittinger, even though the family now owns the restaurant, just a "champagne ordinaire." It is a great idea, say for a buffet lunch with a pitcher of orange juice close by, or how about a plate of julienne lemon peel, orange peel, a bowl of tiny sugar cubes and a bottle of bitters for making a champagne cocktail, a bottle of Cassis for champagne Kirs and a little bucket of ice for those who like it.

The Ideal Kitchen

To envy: a kitchen large enough to hold a small sofa and coffee table where a friend can sit comfortably or for the cook to sit and read while waiting for something to be ready.

Fluorescent lights with one white and one pink so that the cook's skin regains its natural color.

Two nice kitchen colors are celery and cream to replace white, white. And maybe use marine paint; after all it was designed to withstand the abuse of water.

Letter # 14

EARLY SPRING 1985

What one views from the train window is often the backyards of the world; the factory loading area, the parking lot, or maybe the tenement or perhaps a farmer's kitchen garden. Backyards can be very ethnic; one can almost guess from which part of the world the owner comes by what he plants there. If he comes from the warm climates there might be a fig tree or grape arbor. In the country, the viewer sees kitchen gardens and picnic tables under spreading trees, cats and dogs and forgotten tools. The love of the home-grown, the joy of eating something fresh, is everywhere. Look at the potted tomato plant lovingly cared for near the back door or on a city fire-escape. The rider on the train in spring might see an alley cat stretching in the back-stoop sun or early spring bulbs blooming untended by a rusty wire fence.

Waves of Irish immigrants arriving in the New York area over the past hundred years brought with them their love of the soil and the folklore to go with it. One of their cardinal rules has always been that early peas be planted on Saint Patrick's Day even if there is snow. By June, then, there is a crop of sugary early peas. One day while I was shelling peas on our porch overlooking the bay, a child who had come to visit stood transfixed by my work. She said that she did not know that peas came in a pod; all she had ever seen were the ones that came in the box from the freezer.

Fresh Peas

One pound of fresh peas will produce about 1 cup when shelled—enough for two persons. The tenderest peas should be cooked in the gentlest way—in boiling, salted water for four to eight minutes. Keep testing them for doneness. Drain the peas and return them to the pot, shaking them over the heat to remove any remaining moisture. Then add salt, pepper and up to a tablespoon of sugar, depending on their sweetness. Turn into a serving dish and add butter, if you wish.

For larger but still tender peas the following recipe is especially good since the shallots give a more interesting taste than the more generally used pearl onions.

Cook peas as above but add the butter while they are still in the pot. Coat them well with butter and add 3 to 5 tablespoons of minced shallots and continue to cook over a very low heat for five to ten minutes.

Frozen Peas

I give you Julia Child's method of dealing with frozen peas. For two persons, open one box and defrost on the counter until you can separate them with a fork. Meanwhile, in your cooking pot place 1 tablespoon of butter, 1 tablespoon of minced green onions or shallots, and 1 quarter teaspoon of salt, a pinch of pepper and ½ cup of stock. This can be either canned or fresh chicken or mushroom broth or water. Bring to a boil, add the peas, cover and simmer slowly for five or six minutes. Uncover and quickly boil off any remaining liquid. Season, if necessary.

Tips from Thibaut:
Another View of Gourmet Cooking

I am sure most of you have seen that wonderful motion picture, *Out of Africa*, the story of Isak Dinesen's life in Kenya based on her book of the same name. As a result of seeing the film, I have re-read her masterpiece *Seven Gothic Tales*. In one of them, "The Old Chevalier," I found this quote:

"Love with very young people is a heartless business. We drink at that age from thirst, or to get drunk; it is only later that we occupy ourselves with the individuality of our wine. A young man in love is essentially enraptured by the forces within himself. You may come back to that view again in a second adolescence. I know a very old Russian in Paris, enormously rich, who used to keep the most charming young dancers, and who, when once asked whether he had or needed to have, any illusions as to their feeling for him, thought the question over and said: 'I do not think, if my chef succeeds in making me a good omelet, that I bother much whether he loves me or not.'"

If you have not done so recently, re-read these wonderful tales by Isak Dinesen.

—Thibaut de Saint Phalle

Letter Perfect

In this week's mail there was a letter from Mary Weinmann, an old friend from here in Washington, with a new favorite dessert that is not only easy to prepare but can be made a day ahead; plus, it is for only four people, unusual for dessert recipes.

Frozen Ginger-Lemon Mousse

Ingredients:

½ envelope unflavored gelatin

3 tablespoons warm water

½ cup finely chopped preserved ginger (Not crystallized. Look in Chinese section.)

Juice and rind of 1 ½ lemons

Yellow food coloring

2 eggs separated

½ cup sugar

½ cup heavy cream

Dissolve the gelatin in the warm water in a heat-proof container and then place the container in a little simmering water until the gelatin mixture is clear. In a blender, place the lemon juice and ¼ cup of the ginger preserve and puree. With the motor running, gradually add the gelatin. In a large bowl combine the eggs and the sugar and then add the gelatin mixture. Add the remaining ginger, the lemon rind grated, and a few drops of yellow food coloring. Beat the egg whites until stiff and fold in gently but well. Beat the cream until stiff and fold in also. Tie an oiled collar around a 3-cup soufflé mould so that it extends at least 1-inch above the top, and tie. Pour the mixture in and smooth the top. Freeze for at least six hours before serving. Candy flowers (violets look lovely) can decorate the top.

Rosemary

Rosemary is an evergreen and a fairly hardy perennial.

It can survive the cold to about 15°F. It is not at all fussy in its soil requirements but it does require full sun and a dry spot. If possible, plant it on the south side of a masonry wall for better winter protection or it can be potted and brought indoors. Rosemary is an ingredient in many sauces along with parsley, sage, garlic and shallots. In herbal mythology rosemary leaves strewn under your bed will prevent bad dreams, and a plain face can become fair by washing it with an infusion of white wine and rosemary leaves. If you have the patience to wait for it to grow, purchase a pair of hardwood rosemary plants and pot them so that they can be brought into the house in the winter. Pick plants of equal size and stake them and wrap their trunks so that they will form into miniature trees with ball shaped tops. I have seen a pair about eighteen inches high placed on either end of a dining room sideboard in lovely cachepots where they looked beautiful and gave a lovely fresh herbal scent to the room in winter. They have also done well for us in Florida. Plant them to take the morning sun but never in the way of the north wind.

A Culinary Herb Garden

Herbs lend themselves well to pot gardening so that apartment dwellers can have just as successful herb gardens as country gardeners. The essential requirement is a southern exposure. The indispensable dozen herbs that I list below for a very small garden are also just as adaptable to city containers. First pick a sunny location and secondly draw a plot plan noting the colors and shapes and the sizes to which they will mature. In the same way, container sizes should be taken into consideration. Then think about the herbs you tend to use most in your cooking and adjust the number of plants accordingly. Remember that perennial herbs, once planted and cultivated, are permanent plantings so place them in your garden carefully. The annuals should be rotated each year, therefore plant them in a different area but in the same general location. An old and wise Italian gardener convinced me years ago that if you want really fine tasting tomatoes you must plant your basil around each tomato plant (it saves space too).

Parsley: Italian flat leafed and curly. A dozen plants. A perennial except in very cold areas.

Sage: One plant will mature to two feet in diameter. Perennial.

Rosemary: One plant can grow into a sizable bush.

Tarragon: Will grow to two feet in diameter. Perennial.

Oregano: (Wild marjoram) grows two feet tall. Perennial, except in northern climates.

Chervil: Resembles parsley. Six plants. Annual.

Thyme: Thymus Vugaris is the culinary one. Matures to a matted clump of one yard. Perennial. Protect from severe cold.

Garlic: Plant sixty specimen (large) cloves for a years supply. Annual.

Shallots: Same as garlic.

Basil: Six plants. Annual.

Dill: Six plants. Annual.

Chives: Four plants. Annual.

If you have a damp spot, plant some spearmint and if you have a dry rocky place plant the beautiful aromatic lavender. Nasturtiums, of course, are a riot of color and have many culinary uses besides.

Some Thoughts

James Beard's philosophy; "You don't have to go to great pains to be hospitable." How true. Isn't it better to entertain simply but with care than not to entertain at all? Just do not ever apologize for the simple.

Caring and a little taste are sufficient.

The Romans had a phrase for quick action. "In less time than it takes to cook asparagus." It is an indication of just how important vegetables were to them and that they had learned the delicate art of preparing them. In their time, vegetables were not only considered healthy but also as great benefactors. Cabbage was eaten to ward off drunkenness, onions and leeks to build up strength. Mushrooms were so highly thought of that Caesar restricted their sale to the wealthy. Even family names were taken from vegetables: Fabius from Faba (bean); Lenulus from lenticula (lentils).

After the fall of the Roman Empire vegetables lost favor in Europe and, contrary to Europe, colonial Americans made extensive use of vegetables in their menus. Parameter worked at popularizing the potato in France and we exported the tomato to Italy where it has flourished. George Washington's kitchen had every known legume as he was always collecting seeds on his travels or they were brought to him as gifts. Thomas Jefferson returned from his ambassadorial duties in France with broccoli and asparagus seeds to propagate in his greenhouse.

I do not recommend a half-cooked vegetable. Either cook it or leave it raw. From a health standpoint, the oriental diet needs the roughage of a raw vegetable since salads are not eaten—but we do not have that problem. Vegetables, like pasta, should be cooked until, neither overdone nor underdone but al dente.

Spring Lamb

It is that wonderful time of the year when baby lamb comes to the market with baby legs, weighing 6 pounds or less. I believe that the finest way to prepare lamb is to roast it in the French manner and I hope you will agree after trying it.

Ingredients:

6 or 7 pound leg of lamb (Ask the butcher not to remove thin tissue-like covering.)

2 cloves of garlic peeled and cut into slivers

3 tablespoons vegetable oil

2 tablespoons coarse salt

2 large onions thinly sliced

2 large carrots thinly sliced

4 stalks celery cut into one inch pieces

1 ½ cups stock, chicken or beef, canned or fresh

Salt and French ground black pepper

½ teaspoon lemon juice

Preheat the oven to 500°F.

Make small incisions all over the lamb and insert the slivers of garlic. Brush the meat all over with oil or duck fat and then rub it with the salt. Place the leg, fat side up, on a rack in a shallow roasting pan and roast for twenty minutes at 500°F. Then turn the heat down to 350°F, add the cut up vegetables to the pan and continue roasting without basting for maybe fifty to fifty-five minutes longer. Remove the lamb from the oven when the meat thermometer reads 145°F (medium rare). Let the roast rest for fifteen minutes before carving. Now make the sauce. Add the stock to the roasting pan and bring to a boil on top of the stove and let boil for three or four minutes, scraping all the brown off the bottom of the pan. Pour the reduced sauce through a sieve into a saucepan pressing hard on the contents with the back of a spoon in order to extract all the juices. Skim off any fat and add salt, pepper and lemon juice and reheat the sauce, if necessary, before serving.

Traditionally the French serve flageolet beans with their lamb but our white beans work well too. Soak the beans for the required time in cold water. Change the water and cook them slowly until done (look at the package directions for timing), along with a peeled onion stuck with 3 or 4 cloves and some salt. When the beans are cooked, drain them and moisten them with some of the juices from the roasting pan to give a wonderful flavor.

Letter # 15

SPRING, 1985

I move around Washington in the spring and marvel at the beauty of this city. Whether or not it is due to the drought that we are experiencing or some other cause, that matters little; it is a vintage year for the flowering trees; never have they been more breathtaking, and yet they remind me of springtime in another place.

We left Lisbon, Portugal, late one February, bound south by car for the Algarve, eight hours away. It was still winter in Lisbon but I had been promised spring on the other side of the Monchique Mountains and it was so. The mountains were awash in yellow mimosa. We rolled down the windows to fill the car with their perfume. On the south side of the mountain stretches the great plain that is the Algarve, which at that moment was covered with a white blanket of flowering almond trees. The people here tell a story of a long-ago Portuguese king who married a princess from a northern country and brought her to live in the Algarve where the winters are mild. But the princess missed the snow-covered country of winter and, as the king loved his queen and wished to cure her homesickness, he planted almond trees in the fields of the valley and, when they came into bloom in February, and the Queen looked out from her castle on the hill facing the great plain, it looked as though the lands were covered with snow.

In Praise of Spring

Now is the time of the year when the heart and mind move outdoors to the park, picnic table, beach or sunny sidewalk café, out of the winter house and into the warmth of springtime. Out of the car and onto the boat, away from the city and into the tent, out of a gym and onto a bicycle. Menus change to fit the rising temperatures and more leisurely lifestyles. Set your tables with whimsy and plan your meals with a light touch, for we have passed through the Ides of March and into a season of beauty.

To walk through the Impressionist show at the National Gallery is, in fact, more of a walk through the spring of the year. It is not that there are not plenty of examples of other seasons, but one is drawn to those paintings with the flowering trees, freshly-tilled fields and sometimes airily sketched ladies in crispy white batistes. You wish you could spend the day picnicking with them from bulging wicker hampers.

The British are renowned for their ability to live comfortably outdoors under adverse conditions which, I believe, is part of the reason that they were so successful at colonizing in uncomfortable places. It is an attitude about lifestyle. They have always placed considerable emphasis on being very civilized even under the most difficult conditions. My grandfather was a great exponent of living well in the out-of-doors; I have a favorite photograph of my grandparents on a fishing trip in the north woods of Maine. There is my grandfather, Maximillian, holding a black-rimmed, white tin plate of trout he had just sautéed over a driftwood fire, my father standing next to him with a frosty tin shaker of dry martinis ready to be poured. It does not matter that there was not a soul around to observe their lifestyle—they simply thought that making life pleasant does matter. This, of course, can also open up a whole can of worms (an ill-chosen simile for a piece on eating outside). You begin with the children who, they say, shall inherit the earth—what an unsettling thought—but if it is to be, at least we must teach them to do it with style, manners and good taste buds, and all else, I am confident, will fall somehow into place.

Packing the picnic food is just as important as preparing it, so here are some suggestions for having your picnic arrive in the same condition it left your kitchen.

1. Secure tops of all plastic containers with masking tape and turn upside down to test for leakage.

2. Anything that bruises easily should go into a hard-sided container.

3. Wrap anything breakable in the tablecloth or a sweater or towel.

4. Bake food in shapes that are easy to stow in a pack or basket. One pound coffee cans are a good size and shape, and so are the small-size foil loaf pans.

5. Avoid sauces or dips that use eggs since they spoil quite easily if not refrigerated on a hot day.

6. Zip lock bags are extremely useful, filled with all components of a meal.

7. Keep all liquids in screw-top jars. The plastic traveling containers for cosmetics are very good for carrying salt, pepper, sugar, oil, etc.

8. If you are taking a grill, wrap the briquettes in a paper bag, place them inside the grill and then wrap that in a plastic bag and tie. The grill and pans can go back inside for the trip home.

9. Carry whole roasted birds wrapped in a damp cloth, and then place them in a plastic bag. Instead of a carving knife, bring a pair of poultry shears; they are much easier to use since you are not slicing but dividing.

10. If you are not going to be near water, bring hot, damp, rolled cloths, à la Japanese-Chinese restaurants, stored in a plastic bag.

A good practice to follow in the warmer months is to cook in larger quantities when you do cook as the leftovers can be the base for a later cold meal. Cold vegetables and potatoes for salads, cold meats for slicing or salads, rice as well, and purees of vegetables all ready for the addition of cream to become a soup. Extra breads, muffins and rolls wrapped in foil can be thawed in no time in the oven or out in the sun.

Cold Strawberry Soup

Here is an unusual way to use strawberries (which are irresistible to the eye of the shopper; they just scream at you with their scarlet red jackets).

Ingredients:

1 quart fresh strawberries

½ cup unsweetened pineapple juice

1 large ripe peach, peeled, pitted and sliced (1 twelve-ounce package frozen sliced peaches can be substituted).

2 cups strong chicken broth

½ cup sour cream

2 tablespoons chopped toasted almonds

Put half of the strawberries and all the pineapple juice in a blender and puree. Add the rest of the strawberries and the peach and puree.

Pour the broth into a large bowl, add the puree and beat with a wire whisk for a couple of minutes. Chill thoroughly before serving. Float something green, such as a mint leaf, on top of each serving.

Strawberries with Chocolate Sauce

Here is a very easy, very good chocolate dessert. Simply put a scoop of chocolate ice cream on a dessert plate and blanket it with a good, rich, chocolate sauce. Decorate each serving with a giant strawberry, preferably with the stem still on, set to one side.

Chocolate Sauce:

4 squares of bitter chocolate

1 tablespoon of butter

1 cup sugar

1 cup of light cream

1 teaspoon of vanilla

Place the chocolate and the butter in the top of a double boiler and melt over hot water. Combine the sugar and the cream and add to the melted chocolate. Over direct heat, bring the sauce to the boiling point, stirring constantly. Lower the heat and cook a bit longer until the sauce thickens some. Remove from the heat and add the vanilla. Reheat over simmering water. Leftover sauce freezes well and can be reheated in a double boiler.

Snails

Did you know that Americans buy eight hundred and fifty million dollars worth of snails per year? Well some bright person in California must have looked at those figures and decided to explore the possibilities of selling "made in America" snails. This idea delighted the California farmers because they don't like snails and now they have snail pickers running all over their farms gathering up the nasty little things. But there are also those who are now raising snails in climate-controlled greenhouses with specially balanced diets of grains. Escargots are canned in brine or broth in France but the California variety is preserved in water giving it a fresher taste, and it is cheaper too.

Mushrooms Stuffed with Snails

Drain a can of snails and rinse in white wine. Prepare medium-sized mushroom caps for stuffing but do not wash them, simply wipe them off. Prepare snail butter. Place a snail in each cap and cover with the butter mixture and place in a medium oven until just bubbly. Serve them immediately with French bread as a first course. Snail butter is a mixture of soft butter along with minced parsley and garlic.

Snails and Anchovy Butter

Drain and rinse snails as in above recipe. Mix half and half butter and anchovy paste. Place snails in shells or mushroom caps and cover with the butter and anchovy mixture. Heat in the oven until bubbly and serve with French bread.

White Asparagus

We grow the finest green asparagus anywhere, in California. The green asparagus in Europe tends to be pencil thin, so you find the large white instead. Asparagus is naturally green, but if you keep hilling it up as it grows, the sun will never get to the stalk to green it. It is without a suntan. It is absolutely wonderful with a light hollandaise sauce.

Taste without Tears

Because part of the purpose of these letters is to make it easy as possible to eat and drink well alone or with friends in this do-it-yourself world, I have picked at random a few recipes that fit into the delicious, beautiful, unusual, was-this-meal-catered or do-you-have-someone-in-the-kitchen category.

Cherry Tomatoes Stuffed with Avocado

Ingredients:

1 pint cherry tomatoes (30)

2 medium ripe avocados

2 tablespoons sour cream

2 tablespoons minced parsley

4 teaspoons lime juice

2 teaspoons minced chives

2 teaspoons lemon juice

Cut off the tops of the tomatoes, core and drain them upside down on paper toweling. Mince the parsley and chives preferably by hand or in a food processor, and then add the peeled and pitted avocados and the remaining ingredients. The tomatoes can be either filled with a demitasse spoon or the puree can be piped through a pastry tube into the cavities.

Salade au Chapon

Chill a salad bowl and the salad greens. Rub a slice of French bread with the cut side of a garlic clove and sprinkle it with a tablespoon of extra virgin olive oil. Prepare equal amounts of romaine, endive and chicory for a salad, breaking them into small pieces and toss them in the chilled salad bowl with the chapon (bread) and 3 tablespoons of vinaigrette sauce. Remove the chapon before serving the salad.

Dill Vinaigrette

In a small glass or ceramic bowl combine 2 tablespoons of lemon juice, 1 tablespoon of Dijon mustard, ¼ teaspoon sugar and ½ to ¾ cup of virgin olive oil to your taste. It is important to keep whisking as each ingredient is added so that the sauce blends well. Now add 3 tablespoons of fresh chopped dill and salt and pepper to your liking.

String Beans

For two persons take ½ pound of string beans of equal size, the smaller the better. Snip off the ends and place them in a pot with 2 tablespoons of melted butter and stir to coat with the butter. Turn the heat down very low and add lemon juice, pepper, salt and nutmeg to taste. Cover the pan and cook for about six minutes.

Leg of Lamb with Mustard Garlic and Rosemary

Ingredients (serves 8 to 10):

7 ½ pound leg of lamb, boned and rolled

1 ¼ cups Dijon mustard

6 garlic cloves

4 tablespoons fresh rosemary leaves, or 2 tablespoons crumbled dried sprigs of rosemary for garnish (fresh figs if desired)

In a blender or food processor puree the mustard, garlic, rosemary, salt and pepper. Preheat the oven to 450°F and roast the lamb on one side until it is well browned. Coat the seam of the rolled lamb with some of the paste and roast for another ten minutes at a time until the meat thermometer registers 130°F for rare meat. Remove the lamb from the oven and let it rest for ten minutes before carving.

Serve on a platter garnished with fresh rosemary sprigs and accompany with the remaining paste and some figs if you like.

Fish Filets—Le Bernardin

Le Bernardin, the renowned fish restaurant in Paris, has recently opened a restaurant in New York (*www.le-bernardin.com*), and Craig Claiborne interviewed Chef Gilbert Le Coze for the *New York Times*. In the article there were some food tips, such as how to tell when a whole fish is done. Take a cake tester and insert it into the meatiest part of the fish and, when you pull it out, it should be nicely warmed but not too hot to the touch upon your lips. For cooking fillets he uses a non-stick pan into which he puts a tiny bit of oil. When the oil is very hot, at the smoking point, he adds flour-coated fillets and cooks them quickly on each side before removing them to drain their oil on paper towels. Finally, he arranges them on plates and puts them into a preheated 500°F oven for ten to fifteen seconds. What could be simpler? But they will not taste like anything at all if the fish is not the freshest in the market. Chef Le Coze spends three hours each morning at the Fulton Fish Market in lower New York choosing the pick of the catch.

Letter # 16

SUMMER, 1985

This spring is so dry and hot that my usually unsocial land turtle that has lived for years in this little Georgetown garden presented himself on the terrace one recent morning. I was watering ground that was as dry as August when I saw him. I stopped and gave him a piece of gruyère cheese to welcome him back from his (or her) winter hibernation. It was eaten with relish and I paid no further attention and went back to my watering. We ran into each other again halfway inside the back door so I picked him up and gave him a shower from the hose by the back door which he followed with a long, cool drink from the puddles on the terrace. Many Georgetown gardens have families of turtles, and the landscape maintenance men tell me of the garden owners' various instructions for the safety of their turtles. My turtle had a friend for many years but unfortunately it was decapitated by the black cat next door while taking the sun one day on the terrace. It is good to be back outside in summer rooms like shady terraces and cool porches or in soft chairs by breezy open windows. And who can explain why it seems so sensuous to eat under an umbrella?

The Art of Eating Outdoors

If it is not possible to serve a meal or cocktail outside in relative comfort don't even attempt it, as you and your guest will keep trying to sneak back into the house on one pretense or another.

In the warm weather, shade must be provided by one means or another. The meal should always be set out and eaten in the shade unless the day is very cool.

Outdoor lighting should be diffused. It should be placed to show guests how to come and go and to light steps, but tables lit with candlelight can not compete with electric lights which have been set too near. The bulb of a light should never show. One thing is very important and that is the wattage of the light bulb, which should be no more than that of a small reading light, say around twenty-five watts.

A string of white Christmas lights edging a border can give a very pretty effect with little effort. They can also be pushed inside shrubs and hedges to give a glow to the area foliage.

For party lighting, fill the terrace tree with a variety of lighted paper Japanese lanterns, the more the merrier.

When you consider lighting your property for a party, remember that the lighting in the front of the house should not be as bright as the lights at the back where the party will be held. This will give the effect, especially in a small urban garden, of a much greater size. You may want to spray hedges with cold water just before sitting outside as it makes the mosquitoes sleepy.

Hors d' Oeuvre

Martha Stewart's Hors d'Oeuvres Handbook (Clarkson Potter) is full of simple and good foods to serve along with drinks. To be sure, there are many elaborate foods in this book, but if you pick your way through the text there are many practical suggestions. What is also nice is the profusion of photographs illustrating what the final results should look like. This is very helpful. It is a good reference work because the variety of food suggestions will keep it from becoming outdated. Something cool or at room temperature is appealing on a summer evening for accompanying a tall frosty end-of-the-day cocktail.

Marinated Shrimp

Ingredients:

1 pound jumbo shrimp (about 13) either cooked or raw

2 tablespoons of tarragon vinegar

½ cup of olive oil

½ cup of vegetable oil

3 tablespoons of chopped oregano

½ teaspoon of salt and the juice of ½ lemon

If you purchase the shrimps raw, place them in a pot in their shells and barely cover them with water. Bring the shrimp to a boil and turn off the heat. Let them stand a minute for smaller shrimp and a couple of minutes for the larger shrimp, then drain and rinse them thoroughly under cold water. If they are to be stored in the refrigerator for later use, do not shell them until that time.

Shell the shrimp leaving their tails on. Combine all the other ingredients to form a marinade and let the shrimp marinate for three or four hours. Garnish the serving plate with maché or other attractive leafy greens.

Tortellini with Parmesan Lemon Sauce

Ingredients:

1 cup of crème fraîche

¼ cup grated parmesan cheese

Juice of 2 lemons

Grated zest of 2 lemons

3 cloves of roasted garlic, peeled and crushed

1 ½ pounds of the smallest tortellini available

All the ingredients for the sauce can be combined in advance and stored in the refrigerator.

Cook the tortellini in boiling, salted water until just tender, drain and then coat with a touch of olive oil just to keep them from sticking. They can be served at room temperature on tooth picks along with the sauce.

Roasted Garlic

When roasted, garlic becomes sweeter and milder. Preheat oven to 350°F and roast several heads of garlic which have been lightly coated with olive oil for about an hour or until they are golden brown. Separate the cloves and store in a container filled with olive oil.

Crème Fraîche

Crème fraîche is very easy to make if it cannot be found in the market or the price seems unreasonably high.

2 tablespoons buttermilk or sour cream

2 cups heavy cream

Heat the cream to a temperature of 100°F—a good idea but not essential—and mix very thoroughly with the buttermilk. Store in a covered jar at room temperature for six to eight hours and then refrigerate. Do not serve for at least twenty-four hours. Crème fraîche will keep for two or three weeks in the refrigerator. I usually cut the recipe in half because you don't often use more than a cups worth.

Red Potatoes with Sour Cream and Caviar

Find the newest, best, unblemished red skin potatoes all of a size and boil them gently until just tender but not soft. Drain and run under cold water to stop further cooking. Cut the potatoes in half and place cut side up on paper toweling. Using a melon ball scoop, make a hollow in the top of the potato and fill it with sour cream and then top it with the caviar of your choice. Or use finely crumbled fresh bacon, finely chopped scallions, chopped walnuts, or finely chopped fresh herbs.

What To Drink with What

This list is abbreviated but nonetheless gives an idea of what types of wines are known to marry well with certain foods.

Cheese: (soft fermented) St. Emilion, Pommerol

Shellfish: Sylvaner, Muscadet, Pouilly-Fuissé

Fish cooked in Butter or Broiled: Chablis, Sylvaner, Muscadet, Riesling, dry Graves

Fish with Cream Sauce: Montrachet, Meursault, Pouilly Fumé, Tramminer

Roasts

White Meat (Veal and Pork): Red Bordeaux, especially Medocs and St. Estèphe

Red Meat (Filet of Beef and Beef Tournedos): Clos Vougeot, Chambertin, Chambolle, Musigny, (any heavy Burgundy)

Lamb: Chateauneuf du Pape, Clos Vougeot, a light Beaujolais (Moulin-a-Vent)

Chicken: Margaux, Mouton-Rothschild, Volnay,

Moulin-a-Vent

Goose and Duck: St. Julien, St. Emilion, a good Nuits St. George, Chateauneuf du Pape

Turkey: Chateau Lafite, Mouton-Rothschild, Haut Brion, Romanee-Conti

Tips

Tablecloths, unless they are of heavy fabric, really need some kind of a liner under them, especially on outdoor eating tables and plywood party tables. In bygone days flannel liners were cut to fit either under place mats or large cloths. Today it is easier to buy cheap synthetic blankets at discount stores and just cut them to fit. They can be easily washed in a washing machine and lend a nice cushion to the table surface.

Italians feel that vegetables are so important that they often serve them as a separate course. This is a very nice way to serve the beautiful and fresh vegetables of summer. Cooked to perfection they can either be heaped on a platter or composed on individual plates ahead of time. Think of the color combinations that can present themselves and of the light sauces that can be spooned over them. For an outside table the sauce can be served in hollowed out vegetables such as green and red peppers, squashes or artichokes.

The easiest and neatest way to eat a hard boiled egg is to take a piece of sturdy thread and loop it around the egg. As you pull it tight it makes a nice cut through the egg.

Napkins arranged in wine glasses rather than on the plate or table save a lot of space at a tightly set table. Have you ever tried to get up and serve yourself from a densely seated table? It is better to avoid that mistake by serving the guest yourself, if there is no other seating alternative. If at all possible, at a buffet meal set out the main course for everyone to serve themselves and let them stay seated while the plates are taken away and plates of dessert are passed. Conversation has a hard time surviving when one must disappear two or three times in order to help oneself or another guest.

Potatoes for Outdoor Cooking

After you have baked your potato to perfection on the grey coals, as explained earlier, cut an X in the top of the potato and squeeze it open. Serve it as a first course with salt, freshly ground pepper and a pitcher of the richest cream in the market—it will taste so delicious, the cold cream on the hot potato.

Galette Potatoes

This is potatoes Anna done on top of the stove rather than in the oven.

Ingredients:

3 to 4 baking potatoes peeled and thinly sliced

4 tablespoons of butter

Salt and freshly ground pepper

Extra butter

Melt the butter in a heavy skillet which has a tight fitting cover. Arrange the potatoes in a spiral starting in the middle and overlapping out to the edge of the pan. Repeat for two or three layers, adding salt, pepper and pieces of butter between each. Cover the pan, place over medium heat, cook until the potatoes are brown on the bottom and tender. Remove the pan from the heat and leave covered while the meat is grilled. If you like, invert the potatoes onto a tray and slip back in the pan in order to brown the other side. Otherwise, just invert onto a platter at serving time.

If you are now sitting happily under your sensational umbrella, I hope you are about to be served something sensational from the grill.

Letter # 17

SUMMER, 1985

It is summertime, traveling time, and half the fun can be getting there even if it means driving. How about a picnic lunch? Do you stop at the farm stands? Do you ever drive on a secondary road for a change of pace from the four lane strip? An extra hour or a little less mileage can turn a chore into an adventure. Seafood purchased along the coast to present to an inland hostess, a fat chicken, large brown eggs and crispy fresh vegetables to gather on the way to the mountains. Headed to the coast? Take along some maple syrup, some fruits and baby new potatoes to accompany a good fish. Local cheeses and baked goods could wind up your shopping except perhaps for homestyle ice cream and candy from near your destination. Menus develop as the miles tick off. By the time you arrive, you, children, dogs and cats will have stretched their legs a half dozen times, will have experiences to recount and the ingredients for a fine meal in the car. It is helpful to take along a cooler which, after lunch, can be filled with perishables. Are you prepared for finding something delicious around the next bend?

The Statue of Liberty

The Statue of Liberty, as we all know, holds the torch of freedom in her hands, but did you ever stop to think that it also looks like a great big American ice cream cone? Well it came to mind when reading a short article in a recent *Time* magazine entitled "American Best." *Time* interviewed a mixed bouquet of Europeans on what they considered American Best. Janet Morgan from the BBC was quoted as saying "I think Americans are best at making ice cream." Now that is a refreshing summer thought and Janet Morgan is absolutely correct, we do make great ice cream and maybe at this time of rededication it is in our own best interest to think a little about all the products that we do make or could make *best*. We have a lot to be proud of that is uniquely ours and excellent. After all, have you read anything regarding dairy herds in Japan producing the rich milk and cream we have in our fair land?

When I think of ice cream, I think of New England where the ice cream "shoppe" has always been the biggest treat in town. The parlors are traditionally sparkling white inside and often outside too, and for some reason I have never been able to fathom, the further north one goes the more popular they are, and the ice cream is superb.

Fresh Peach Sauce

From a 1972 gourmet magazine:

Place 1 cup of fresh sliced peaches, the same amount of ice cream and ¼ cup of rum into the container of a blender and puree until smooth. Serve over fresh fruit.

Butterscotch Sauce

From *American Cookery* by James Beard

Ingredients:

1 ⅓ cups dark brown sugar

¾ cup light corn syrup

3 tablespoons of butter

2 tablespoons of water

3 to 4 tablespoons of heavy cream

In a heavy saucepan bring all the ingredients, except for the cream, to a boil. Boil for one minute, stirring and then cool for twenty minutes before adding the cream. Stir until the sauce is smooth and satiny.

This is real butterscotch sauce where the sauce turns chewy when it makes contact with the cold ice cream.

Ice Cream at State

Apparently foreign guests at the State Department agree with our earlier comments for they love to be served ice cream. According to a Chief of Protocol, Selma Roosevelt, in an issue of *Vogue*,

"All foreigners seem to love ice cream." Ambassador Roosevelt, (her husband is Archibald Roosevelt of the Oyster Bay Roosevelts) often serves pumpkin or mango ice cream with chocolate shavings.

Outdoor Grilling

Why not light the grill and cook dinner outdoors tonight. Here is a dinner fit for four:

Lamb Chops with Fresh Rosemary Provencial

Ingredients (serves 4):

4 two-inch thick loin lamb chops

4 ten-inch rosemary branches

Marinade:

2 anchovy fillets drained and dried

2 medium cloves of garlic

6 fresh rosemary leaves (¼ teaspoon dried)

Salt

1 tablespoon dry red wine

3 tablespoons good green olive oil

Either with a pestle and mortar or with a large, sharp, heavy knife, or mini food processor, chop the dry ingredients and then stir in the wine and oil. Now make 2 shallow incisions in each chop and rub the marinade thoroughly into them. Let the chops stand in the marinade for at least an hour at room temperature before grilling. Tie the chops securely with string and wrap the rosemary branches around the chops and secure with string. Brush a little olive oil on the grill and place the meat over hot, gray coals, grilling for six minutes on one side before turning and testing until they are done to your liking.

Wild and Brown Rice Salad with Olives

This salad can be made the day before and brought back to room temperature before serving.

Ingredients:

¾ cup wild rice

¾ cup brown rice

(or you can buy Uncle Ben's wild rice and brown rice mixture and discard the seasoning packet or save for using with your own white rice)

¼ cup wine vinegar

½ cup olive oil

½ cup pimento stuffed green olives (large, sliced)

⅓ cup minced scallions

¼ cup minced parsley leaves (preferably Italian)

In a pot of rapidly boiling salted water place the well rinsed wild rice and boil for fifteen minutes. Add well rinsed brown rice and boil for another fifteen minutes and drain and rinse under cool water. (For Uncle Ben's follow their cooking directions.) Set the rice in a colander covered with a dish towel and lid over some boiling water and let steam gently for fifteen or twenty minutes until the rice is light and fluffy. Stir in the rest of the ingredients with two forks and add salt and pepper to taste. Refrigerate the salad when it cools, if necessary, but be sure to serve it at room temperature.

For a first course, skewered fish can be cooked on the grill before the coals are gray enough for the chops. The following is from *Martha Stewart's Hors d'Oeuvres Handbook*.

Grilled Swordfish with Cherry Tomatoes

Ingredients:

½ pound fresh swordfish cut ¾-inch thick and then cut into cubes

¼ cup olive oil

1 tablespoon fresh fennel leaves

½ pint cherry tomatoes

Marinate the swordfish cubes in the oil and fennel leaves for at least two hours. Halve the cherry tomatoes and put on the skewers, alternating with 2 cubes of fish. They will only need a couple of minutes grilling over hot coals. Serve them immediately.

The dinner is complete with a cool dessert such as a fresh fruit with the peach sauce mentioned earlier and a salad and cheese course, if you wish.

Book Review

French Cooking in Ten Minutes is a translation and reprint of a publication *La Cuisine Dix Minutes*. It is published in this country by Farrar, Straus and Giroux and is filled with charming pen and ink drawings that were done for the original by Andre Giroux. The author was Edouard de Pomaine, a doctor at the Institute Pasteur who, according to the introduction, "combined his interest in the scientific and the sensual in a study which he christened 'Gastro technology.'" That is a simply awful word—so pay no attention to it—and continue to read this useful, amusing and attractive book by one of France's best known food writers. Some examples:

"The first thing you must do when you get home, before you take off your coat, is to go to the kitchen and light the stove . . .

"Next, fill a pot large enough to hold a quart of water.

"Put it on the fire, cover it, and bring it to a boil. What's the water for? I don't know but it's bound to be good for something . . ."

On eggs: "It takes two to scramble. That's why we always make scrambled eggs, not scrambled egg."

On soup: "Can a soup be prepared in ten minutes? Certainly, if you follow a few guidelines. The longest part is bringing two cups of water to a boil. But that time doesn't count, since before we started cooking we put a pot of water on the stove.

"I am writing a book for students, dressmakers, secretaries, artists, lazy people, poets, men of action, dreamers, scientists, and everyone else who has only an hour for lunch or dinner but still wants thirty minutes of peace to enjoy a cup of coffee."

Newsletter 18

LATE SUMMER, 1985

Lifestyles, "Savoir Vivre," is the aesthetic awareness that brings comfort to a place, contentment to the eye, and taste to the palate. Really, it is possible to turn a pumpkin into a carriage: just move things around or paint the walls or take down the curtains. Americans seem to be increasingly conscious of the value of leisure time and see the quality of those hours as an important part of their lives. This awareness comes in part, I am sure, from the exposure to different lifestyles through increased travel and goes hand in hand with the growing interest in this country's cuisine.

I quote here a few observations on the aesthetics of life:

> *William Lyon Phelps:*
> "There is a strange reluctance on the part of most people to admit that they enjoy life."
>
> "To live remains an art which everyone must learn, and which no one can teach."
>
> *Vita Sackville-West:*
> "To the Italians, style is religion; to the British it is class. To the French, style means quality of life—as basic to happiness as the smell of fresh bread in the morning. It's not how much money one makes, but how well one eats that counts.

"That Gallic set of priorities comprises the French "Art de Vivre"—literally, the art of living—which puts all aesthetic pleasure on a pedestal."

Peaches Cardinal

A good news broadcast ends with an upbeat story and so should a meal end with a bit of whimsy that brings a smile, an amusing story and a delightful dessert! This recipe will serve eight people.

Ingredients (serves 8):

8 large ripe peaches

2 ½ cups sugar

5 cups cold water

4-inch piece of vanilla bean or

3 tablespoons of pure vanilla extract

2 packages of frozen raspberries, defrosted

2 tablespoons of very fine sugar

1 tablespoon kirsch

¾ cup of heavy cream

Chopped pistachio nuts for garnish

Well ahead of time, or the day before, drop the peaches into a pot of boiling water for about thirty seconds, remove with a slotted spoon and run them under cold water, to cool them just enough for peeling. Bring the water, sugar and vanilla bean to a boil in a large pot, stirring until the sugar dissolves, and let boil three minutes before turning the heat down to a simmer and adding the peaches. Poach them slowly for ten to twenty minutes until they are tender but not soft. Chill them well.

Drain the defrosted raspberries well, puree through a strainer and add the sugar and the kirsch. Cover the puree with Saran wrap and refrigerate.

Before serving dinner, place a peach on each dessert plate or on one large platter and pour the raspberry puree over them. Either pipe or spread the cream, whipped until stiff with the sugar and the vanilla extract added at the half-way point, and pipe a ring around the fruit. Sprinkle with a few chopped pistachio nuts and refrigerate until time for dessert.

The name *cardinal* comes from the fact that the peach is wearing a hat as red as a cardinal's.

Peach Pie

Ingredients:

5 cups of peeled, sliced peaches

1 baked 9-inch pie shell

1 teaspoon lemon juice

1 tablespoon sugar

1 tablespoon cornstarch

1 tablespoon sweet butter

Topping:

¾ cups white or light brown sugar

1 cup flour

¼ pound softened sweet butter

1 teaspoon cinnamon

Peel and slice the peaches and place in a bowl with the lemon juice, cornstarch and the sugar. Mix thoroughly but gently and then place in the baked pie shell and dot with the butter. Cover the pie with the topping and bake at 400°F for twenty-five to thirty minutes.

Serve with ice cream or whipped cream flavored with a little cognac.

Gourmet's Garden

Because it is now the beginning of the harvest season, I have asked Kit Casper to write about vegetable farming. Kit was a ski instructor at Saddleback Mountain in northern Maine when he and his pretty young wife, Linda, decided to buy some land and an old farm house and began to raise vegetables and flowers in between snow seasons. It took them several years to manually clear the rocks from their fields but today they have a very successful and sophisticated farm garden hidden in a wilderness region forty miles, as the crow flies, from Quebec Province, Canada.

One is handicapped in the northern woods by poor soil, rocks, roots, stumps and a minimal growing season in a latitude that does not take too kindly to many varieties of vegetables and flowers. My grandfather wrote a book entitled *And the Wilderness Blossomed* on building a garden in the north and he would have been astonished at what this farm has produced and the quality of its products.

Linda is responsible for the buckets of old fashioned flowers and herbs for sale in the shed, and Kit's bouquets of vegetables are a cook's dream. Here is his article.

> Small vegetables are not only trendy but incredibly delicious. If you have the fortune of even a small garden with good light, growing them requires mostly extra care and attention.
>
> Start by considering the soil. Light, spongy soil loaded with organic matter will produce vegetables that grow quickly and taste marvelous. Rich organic soil holds many nutrients to be released as the plants need them. It also holds an abundance of water: the best vegetables are grown with a steady supply of water rather than the feast or famine regimen nature often supplies.
>
> Work your soil well so it has a fine, smooth crumb texture, particularly where root crops are to grow. Thin religiously so each plant has its own space, though in truth most vegetables can be grown closer than gardening books recommend since they will be harvested long before reaching maturity. Weed regularly, for there are only so many nutrients and so much

water to go around and you want the whole bounty available for your vegetables.

And watch closely! Plants growing in optimum conditions change very rapidly. Don't let them get too big. Freshly picked carrots the size of your little finger, beets like a quarter, zucchini with the blossoms still full at the tip will bring to your plate and palate a treat reserved for those who can grow their own. Keep the time between harvests and eating to the barest minimum, for every moment brings some loss of texture and flavor.

My father's recipe for corn on the cob went this way: "Put salted water on to a boil; when it is hot, pick and husk the corn; run with it to the kitchen; if you trip and fall on the way, discard the corn and go back for some that is fresh."

Hints

Don't pull back the husk to inspect the corn in the market; it will start to lose its sugar quickly; simply take home a couple of extra ears.

All lettuce should be washed and drained well as soon as it is purchased, then wrapped in a damp kitchen towel and put in a plastic bag for storage. It will store longer and stay crisper and this is especially true with hydroponic lettuce which becomes nice and crisp, making it more like field lettuce.

When choosing a melon for ripeness, look for one with the yellowest skin as it has had more sun. If it still has some stem on it, it was picked too soon. Beware of melons with no sweet scent.

Grilled Duck

This is my adaptation or simplification of the Chinese procedure for a crisp duck. In China, one always purchases a duck with its head still attached in order to keep it as air tight as possible for blowing air between the skin and meat. Also, the brain and tongue are considered a great delicacy. A Long Island duck is a direct descendent of the Peking duck and is an excellent substitute.

The day before your duck dinner, rinse and drain the duck and massage the whole bird by rubbing the skin back and forth to loosen the skin from the meat. Bring 3 to 4 quarts of water to a boil in a large pot. Tie a sturdy string around the skin on the neck end of the duck leaving a length of about twenty-four inches on both ends. You can also fashion a hook from a wire hanger and put it through the neck bone. Now dunk the duck in and out of the boiling water, ladling water over any exposed skin for about five minutes or until the skin is white and has a dull look. The next step is to hang the duck in a drafty place, with paper underneath, for about six hours. Do not hang it in direct sunlight.

The first time I tried this technique I hung my duck from the Japanese Cherry tree out in my Washington garden. The tree is on the highest level of the garden and so the duck was in full view of my neighbors and garnered appropriate comments about the de Saint Phalles' culinary preferences.

It is now six hours later and you melt 2 tablespoons of honey in 1 cup of boiling water and then paint this mixture all over your hanging duck, coating it well. Give it another four to six hours of hanging; I find it wise to take it down before cocktail time on the terrace. Your duck should look creamy brown and be parchment dry. Wrap it and store it in the refrigerator overnight.

For roasting the duck in an oven, roast at 425°F on each side for fifteen minutes and then for one hour upright at 350°F. For a browner crust raise the temperature to 375°F for ten or fifteen minutes at the end. Be sure to cover the wing tips with foil.

On the grill you can either roast it whole in a shallow pan or in pieces, with the top down. Start with a hot fire and lower the fire after browning. Do keep testing so that the meat does not get overcooked.

Serve the duck with scallion strips and Hoisin sauce. A vegetable such as eggplant or shredded cabbage and carrots stir-fried at the last minute on the grill makes a wonderful main course. All of it tastes good at room temperature too.

Tips from Thibaut: A Meal to Remember

During World War II, when I served behind the Japanese lines in China (courtesy of the U.S. Navy and General Chennault) with a group of former pirates on a remote peninsular between Canton and Fukien province, I was sometimes invited to a very special feast for some passing dignitary. The cooks would try to fetch a particularly large fish, thirty to sixty pounds and, in accordance with our own ideas of cooking, cut off its head. Unfortunately, the body of the fish was then eaten in the kitchen while the head, in all its glory, was served on a bed of herbs to the guests. Since I was frequently the guest of honor, the staring eye would be taken out of its socket by my host and placed on the rice in my bowl. It has taken me a long time to learn to appreciate oysters again but now that I have become an oysterman in Chincoteague, Virginia, and raise sturgeon in the Tennessee River Valley, I think of these early gastronomic adventures with some sense of nostalgia. After all, in Chincoteague, the fishermen who supplied mussels to a processing plant in the island woods in the early thirties were told they were making munitions there.

—Thibaut de Saint Phalle

Summer Table

Summer tables can be set anywhere, in the breeze or out of it, to have a view in the sun or shade or inside away from the bugs. In any event these evenings are generally less formal, with the emphasis on coolness and comfort. It makes one a little ill at ease when asked to appear without a coat and a tie only to be seated at an ornate table. You and the table are incompatible. The following are a few nice ideas.

A thin slice of lemon on the side of the water glass, especially when using city water.

A cinnamon stick and a slice of orange in the tea glass with mint leaves in the ice cubes.

Terra cotta pots are excellent wine coolers. Plug the hole with a cork and refrigerate ahead of time half full of cold water. On a buffet table the pots can hold baguettes or fruit or whatever strikes your fancy. They are quite decorative.

Quote

"We must draw a very clear distinction between style and decoration. I could consider no modern garden even remotely interesting as a work of art unless it could stand as such, stripped of every single purely decorative attribute."

—Russell Page, *The Education of a Gardener*

Trends

In New York City a fair number of restaurants have chosen to rename themselves with traditional French names and to offer a French menu. The difference is that the food is lighter than the former days (pre-California cuisine). What a delicious thought!

Letter # 19

EARLY FALL, 1985

All day the air has been like damp cotton insulating us from fresh air and clean sounds. Life has become muffled, reminding me of the soft sounds in a theater just before the curtain rises. No one slept well last night, tossing and turning and waking from unsettled dreams, the body sensing, I believe, a change in the hot, sunny, salty summer weather on the outer banks of Virginia.

Our native instincts were true, of course, as we heard by chance around noon that little hurricane Charlie was peeking around Cape Hatteras ready to skip up the coast this afternoon.

I sit on my "look-out porch" facing southwest down the great salt marshes which stretch to the horizon and watch and wait in an eerie, too-early dusk. Below me, diamond back turtles are slipping noiselessly across the estuary to take shelter within the grasses, and the sea birds have all gone into hiding, leaving a giant hole of silence where their conversation generally resides. The crab traps (known here as crab hotels) were hauled up beside the bulkhead to provide a pre-storm lunch before being stored away. It is six p.m. and the tide has flowed into its high-water mark, with two hours time still on its hands to fill to overflowing the water roads from the sea.

There is no wind, no sun and no sound and yet with my binoculars I can see the surf breaking over the dunes of Assateague, monster seas seen without a sound track.

The curtain is about to go up.

—

Meanwhile, lets freeze a quiche. Earlier this year the *New York Times* ran an article on how to make a quiche that can be prepared ahead and frozen successfully so that it retains its original texture. Here is the trick, as well as a recipe from author-teacher John Clany, and it works. The quiche filling is poured into a baked pie shell and frozen immediately. The baking is done later.

Mushroom Quiche

Ingredients (serves 8):

1 baked 9-inch pie shell

2 tablespoons of butter

2 tablespoons of finely chopped shallots

¾ pound thinly sliced mushrooms

3 large eggs

1 ¾ cups heavy cream

½ teaspoon of salt

¼ teaspoon of freshly ground pepper

Melt the butter in a heavy saucepan and add the shallots, stirring and cooking gently until they are transparent. Add the sliced mushrooms, cover and cook for eight minutes. Remove the cover and raise the heat, and continue to cook the mushrooms until the liquid has disappeared. Remove the mixture to a plate to cool.

When the mixture is cool, pour it into a cool baked pie shell and place in the freezer while you beat the remaining ingredients in a large bowl. Spread this mixture on top of the mushroom in the pie shell and then sprinkle with the following ingredients:

2 tablespoons of grated parmesan cheese

2 tablespoons of chopped parsley

2 tablespoons of butter cut into small pieces

Place the quiche back in the freezer, wrapping it up only after it has frozen.

To Bake: Preheat the oven to 375°F and remove the quiche from the freezer, unwrap and place immediately in the oven and bake until it is a golden color, about fifty-five minutes.

Mayonnaise

These are two very foolproof dressings that take but a minute to make in a blender.

Plain Mayonnaise

In a blender container, place 2 large eggs, ½ cup of olive oil, ½ teaspoon of dry mustard and the same of salt along with ⅛ teaspoon of pepper. Cover the container and turn the motor on high.

Remove the cover and very gradually add 1 ½ cups of olive oil in a steady stream. Turn off the motor when the oil is gone and store the mayonnaise in the refrigerator. If you are using a strong (green) oil you might want to use part vegetable oil.

Green Mayonnaise

In a blender container, place ¼ cup of olive oil, 2 tablespoons of wine vinegar, 1 tablespoon of chopped chives, 1 tablespoon of chopped dill, 1 teaspoon dry mustard, ½ teaspoon salt and ½ a clove of garlic, if desired. Cover the container and turn the motor on low and slowly add ¾ cup of olive oil in a steady stream. Turn off the motor when finished and store in the refrigerator. If it does not look quite green enough add a drop of food coloring. Serve with cold fish and shellfish.

Building a Nest

In a recent *Agricultural Digest* there appeared a few observations of Gene Moore, the man who has done the magnificent Tiffany windows for thirty years. They are beautiful vignettes, drawing far more attention then the giant glass display windows on the neighboring buildings.

"Mood not size, is at the heart of comfort."

"Clearance is one word I frequently use—for cutting through the undergrowth of possessions."

Every grownup should have a nest, because how you live is a direct reflection of how you view yourself. It is even more important if you live alone because it is wonderful to be able to come home to a happy, inviting and attractive room, apartment or house. We usually begin to put the first room together with too few objects to fill its space and end up years later with too many. If one is young and poor it is no reason to live in empty spaces. There are many ways to build a room or even an area within a room. Take, for example, a place to sit and eat. Whether it is a dining room or a corner of another room, it can start out with a table and four chairs. Now they can be antiques but that is not at all necessary. My favorite room in Monet's house at Giverny is the dining room. Now there is not a thing of great value in the room, simply built-in cabinets and an enormous table surrounded by chairs. But what makes this room so memorable is that everything in the room is painted in yellow and white and the yellow is the most pure, clean yellow you have ever seen. And on the table sits a simple set of china in the same colors. All it took was paint. Years ago I went to visit a friend of mine in her first house. The thing that she showed me with greatest pride was the dining room table. It had been taken from her grandmother's house where it had lived in the servants dining room. It was oval and chunky and in perfect condition. No one wanted it, and my friend took it because she had not been able to buy a dining room table. She took the table home and gave it three coats of pale green gloss paint, and did the same with the chairs that came with it. It looked smashing. If you don't have a sideboard, attach two wooden or metal arms to the wall and top it with a piece of thick glass or buy a bureau, old or new, and put a top on it. Book shelves, bought or made and painted the same color as the walls, look built-in and increase the perception of room height when taken to the ceiling.

Choices: fill them with books or buy a set of decorative plates and stand them up on the shelves. Plates are a very nice substitute for paintings when hung on the wall. Just remember, for birthdays ask for something for yourself but for Christmas ask for something to decorate the home.

Hints

A good bachelor cook I knew always used Swedish pancake mix when preparing his blueberry pancakes. Wet the pan with cold water to keep milk from sticking to the bottom.

Dampening a slightly old baguette before warming it in the oven makes it fresher.

Good looking kitchen towels make excellent buffet napkins since they will cover the whole lap.

Simonetta

In 1967 Doubleday published a little cookbook written by the Italian fashion designer Simonetta. Her interest in cooking, according to the fly leaf, stemmed from her confinement as a political prisoner in Abruzzi, Italy, during the war. Suffering from boredom, she started to haunt the kitchen of the inn and became fascinated with the world of cuisine. The book was originally intended to be "A small guide for people who haven't any servants but who love whipping up amusing, fun dishes." It grew beyond that, with her increasing enthusiasm for the subject. I will give some recipes from Simonetta's favorite chapter, the one on pasta, dubbed "The *clou* of the Book" (the clou meaning the heart or crux). The book is titled

"A Snob in the Kitchen."

Spaghetti with Saffron

Ingredients (serves 6):

1 tablespoon salt

½ pound spaghetti

1 teaspoon saffron

2 tablespoons butter

2 garlic buds finely chopped

Grated parmesan cheese

In a large pot bring plenty of salted water to a boil. When boiling throw in the spaghetti and the saffron. Cook for eight to ten minutes, drain and add the butter and garlic and serve at once.

Spaghetti Sicilian Style

Ingredients:

1 cup raisins

3 tablespoons oil (1 for water and 1 for mixing)

2 tablespoons salt

1 ½ pounds spaghetti

1 cup pignoli (pine nuts)

½ cup capers

1 cup seedless black olives cut in half

8 anchovy fillets cut into small pieces

Soak the raisins in water for a couple of hours to inflate them. Add 1 tablespoon of oil to a large pot of boiling water and add the spaghetti.

Cook until it is just "al dente." Drain and add all the remaining ingredients, including the raisins which have been drained and dried with toweling. Lightly butter a heavy frying pan and add the spaghetti mixture, mashing it down with a spatula. Sauté over medium heat until a nice brown crust has formed on the bottom, turning it over and browning the other side. Serve immediately.

Some additional comments from Simonetta: "If accessories are the sauces and salads of couture, and evening dresses the dessert, then what is the menu but the all important combination of everything to give a whole look: An arrangement of exotic fruits and nuts always makes a charming centerpiece for a cozy table setting . . . I always wander around my house opening drawers and cupboards to find inspiration in some unusual object for the centerpiece in my table setting."

Napkins and a Trout Stream

I came across a man who must be one of the world's great napkin folders. He is the English butler to friends and while we visited with them in the remotest part of the Catskill Mountains, Leslie demonstrated, meal after meal, his beautiful designs. He claims to have one hundred and fifty different ways to set a napkin on a table. Some he learned and a great many he has invented. Each has a lovely name, such as "rose in bloom," "tulip," and "butterfly." A French gentleman houseguest has been trying to get him working on a book of his designs and maybe he will.

This particular part of the Catskills was the birthplace of Jay Gould and many years after he left to make his fortune, he returned and bought a great tract, a whole mountain of streams and small farms. He had a sickly son and thought that the clear mountain air would be healthful for him. He built a large stone-and-wood "camp" in the style of the day but never really stayed there himself. His children and grandchildren loved the summer life there and have continued to hold onto, improve and increase their properties. There are three miles of a beautiful trout stream which runs down from the mountain toward the Delaware River. The stream has never been stocked and is treated as a great treasure and responsibility. Frequently picnics are planned on the flat rock ledges by the cold blue pools. This stream sends water to New York City, but you would never know it was the same water by the time it reaches the drinking glass on the city restaurant tables where it smells more like chemicals than water from a mountain stream.

Letter # 20

FALL, 1985

Pierre's Latest: Won Ton Ravioli

Dear Pierre Franey has done it again: he has found out how Christian Delouvrier, the chef at the Hotel Meridian in New York, makes his thinner-than-thin ravioli. It is ingeniously simple, as most good ideas are. Monsieur Delouvrier uses won ton skins purchased from local Chinese markets, but they can also be found at supermarkets. Why are they so good? Because they are more thinly and evenly rolled than you could probably do yourself, which also means that they are exceedingly light. They can be filled with leftover meat or vegetables which have been finely minced and seasoned. Or how about truffles, paté or cheese or shellfish? The procedure for preparing them follows. A sauce can be poured over but keep it light.

The won ton wrappers must be stored in an airtight container in the freezer or refrigerator. When you are preparing the won ton wrappers, be sure to keep the ones that you have waiting under a damp towel.

1. Place one skin on a dry surface that has a light dusting of flour and paint the skin with an egg wash (1 egg beaten with a couple of drops of water).

2. Place a small spoonful of filling in the center.

3. Place a second skin on top and crimp (squeeze) the edges together so that the filling is sealed in.

4. Trim off the excess dough with a knife or pasta cutter.

5. Place the prepared skins on a dry towel and cover with plastic wrap until cooking.

6. Bring a generous amount of salted water to a boil and cook the ravioli without crowding until they rise to the surface, which means they are done.

Drain and serve—Bravo

Mariana's Chicken and Goat Cheese Ravioli

6 per person

Filling (serve 6 per person):

Diced cooked chicken breast (very fine)

Softened goat cheese, enough to bind the filling

A generous amount of minced fresh tarragon

Salt and pepper

Sauce:

For 2 persons

2 tablespoons of butter

1 cup of half and half

2 thin slices of prosciutto ham, thinly julienned

1 tablespoon of sherry

Melt the butter and add the half and half which has been warmed and then the beaten egg yolk, and stir until it has slightly thickened. Now add the ham and the sherry, some pepper, and heat but do not boil the sauce.

Fraises Du Bois

Fraises du bois are alpine strawberries, tiny and tart with a strong perfume. They make an excellent border plant and do well in containers. They are delicious to eat and produce most of the summer. They are superb in a tart. In California, plant them in the fall, but in the cooler climates wait until early spring. Buy a minimum of fifty plants in order to have a decent harvest. They do best with afternoon shade and prefer rich, well-drained soil.

Rosemary

A new, more hardy strain of rosemary has been recently put on the market called Arp rosemary. It can be ordered from herb farms. It is known to be able to survive winter outdoors as far north as Boston. The flowers are pale blue and the scent is a little piney.

Rosemary survives best when planted in front of a wall with southern exposure to protect it from the north winds in the winter. You must mulch it well in the winter months and provide good drainage. Containers of rosemary must come indoors in the winter, except in zones 9-10.

Good Ideas

Make some homemade mayonnaise using sesame seed oil.

All oils should be stored in dark containers.

Sesame Oil Vinaigrette

Ingredients:

1 teaspoon of dry mustard

1 clove of garlic (optional)

1 ½ teaspoons of lemon juice

Salt and pepper

¼ cup of sesame seed oil

Mix the dry mustard with a few drops of water in order to make a paste and let it stand for a few minutes to age. Add all the other ingredients except for the oil and blend. Slowly whisk in the oil. This dressing is very good on cold vegetables. If they are available cooked and chilled, Chinese long beans are a very attractive salad with this dressing.

Mix and Match

The Italian houseware designers have brought out a new concept in cooking pots and pans. It is perfectly simple to go out and buy a matched set of cookware, which is just fine, but what if you like to fry an egg in an iron skillet, make your crepes in black steel and your sauces in copper? Alessi of Italy (www.alessi.com) has put together a twenty-three piece cooking set (pieces can be bought separately) called the Belt of Orion. I have no idea where they got that name. They have combined steel, black steel, copper and stainless steel and have been blessed by the family roster of French chefs.

Grilled Ham, Cheese and Leek Sandwich

This recipe is from the "If You Have to Watch Football at Least Eat Well at Half Time" department. The eating requirement for a television football luncheon is ease of consumption, not to mention ease of preparation. Present the meal on large plates with large napkins and avoid knives if you can. This recipe is from *Cook's Magazine.*

Ingredients (for 4 sandwiches):

4 leeks

6 tablespoons of butter

Salt and pepper

¾ pounds of Port Salut, Muenster or Brie thinly sliced

8 slices of firm, thick bread

⅓ pound of thin sliced prosciutto or ½ pound of smoked ham

Cut the leeks in half lengthwise and remove all but 2 inches of the green stalk. Wash thoroughly and cut into very thin slices. Sauté the leeks in 2 tablespoons of butter until they just begin to turn color. Add 1 cup of water, salt and pepper, and simmer for ten minutes or until tender. Set aside.

Layer half of the bread with half of the cheese slices and then add the ham and leeks. Top with the remaining cheese and bread slices.

Sauté the sandwiches in the remaining butter until they are golden on both sides.

Winter Vegetable Beef Soup

This soup is another great football meal. It is whole meal in a bowl and is even better if made a couple of days before the game. It also freezes very well.

Ingredients:

2 tablespoons of butter

1 pound of ground lean beef

1 garlic clove minced

3 cups of beef stock (fresh or canned beef bullion)

2 large tins of Italian peeled tomatoes

1 cup of each diced:

Potatoes

Celery

Green beans

Carrots

1 cup of dry red wine

2 tablespoons of chopped parsley

½ teaspoon of basil

¼ teaspoon of thyme

Salt and pepper

In a soup kettle, cook the onions in the butter until they turn golden. Stir in the meat and garlic and cook, separating until brown. Add all the other ingredients and bring the soup to a boil. Reduce the heat and cook at a slow simmer for one and one-half hours.

Fettuccini with Caviar

Ingredients (serves 4):

½ pound of fettuccini

½ stick (½ cup) unsalted butter softened

1 cup heavy cream

⅛ teaspoon each of grated nutmeg and cayenne

¾ cup freshly grated parmesan cheese

6 teaspoons of caviar

Cook the fettucini in boiling salted water until done to your liking, and then drain and return it to the cooking pot. Add the butter, the seasonings and the cream and cook two minutes, just to warm. Remove from the heat and stir in the parmesan cheese with two forks. Divide the fettucini between four heated soup plates and bless each serving with 1 ½ teaspoons of caviar. Serve at once and hand out forks and large spoons for eating.

Mirror Image

Why not reflect your new fabulous surroundings in mirrors. Every improvement you make in your environment becomes a double improvement. You will have two pretty gardens as one will be an impression of the other, two sunny windows, two candles instead of one, and two of you! Mirroring is for sparkle and for adding space and glamour.

Hang sconces on mirror—incredible.

Hang paintings on mirrors—comme les Francais.

Hang mirrors, if you can find one, with a mirror frame—sensational—or even an old mirror in an ornate gilt frame.

Mirror the dining room ceiling—especially if the room is dark. It will double the sparkling candlelight coming from the table.

Hang a chandelier from a mirrored ceiling.

Mirror your tiny bathroom, if you have the courage.

A lightweight smoky plastic mirror cut to fit a party table with the cloth underneath and no place mats looks very sophisticated.

Mirror your bedroom ceiling—for fun.

What is "Style"?

What exactly does it mean to do something "with style?" Look back at the places where you have most enjoyed eating, reading, or being entertained—they had to have an appealing atmosphere of some kind, and it did not depend on the amount of money lavished on them. To reduce my thoughts to simple terms, think about walking down the corridor of a college dormitory and looking into the open doors; the rooms are all the same shape and size, but, oh, the difference in the way they are treated. Some are simply a place to change clothes and sleep, but there are others which are so ingeniously put together with odd possessions, like a patchwork quilt, and a room with style is created, drawing the life of the dormitory to its door. Living well means simply having knowledge of what makes the difference, what makes a meal appealing, a garden more beautiful, or a dress move from ordinary to something special. There is a great deal of style all over the world, wonderful ideas just waiting for you to come along and pick them up and put them into your life!

Corsica under Sail

As I write, little white sails on bright colored boards race across in the Gulf of Sapone far below. Beyond are shadows of shoreline seen through the summer haze. A picnic lunch on the beach is planned before the long drive along the coast to Ajaccio, birthplace of Napoleon.

Ajaccio is two cities with the old resting on the harbor and the new rising behind. Dinner is on a terrace near the sea—a little bistro north of a town called "Maxim's." The return, after eating, is to a sultry summer city teeming with tourists, mostly French.

We wake to the winds of the mistral which had slipped in during the early light after a night which was so clear and calm, with a full moon lighting the bay. This is the day to take possession of a chubby little sloop which will be our home for a week. The day is spent stocking the boat with food and wine as the weather becomes progressively worse. So here we rest with the wind and rain and the big black clouds which have blocked out the mountains. We stay moored to the quay for two days with the wind shouting loudly in the rigging. Finally we wake up this morning to less wind, grey clouds and, being Sunday, bells ringing all over town. Departing after lunch, we leave the harbor with a double reef in the main and a working jib. Now there is a little sun as it begins to clear. Outside the harbor there is much more sea than wind, so we take out the two reefs and sail to a small cove in a bay south of Ajaccio to spend the night. A swim is followed by rum cocktails and grilled steak washed down with a nice Corsican vin rouge.

The next morning finds a big sea running, as the sails are raised and trimmed to run down the coast to the ancient city of Bonifaccio. Lunch along the way is of a salty Corsican ham and crusty coarse bread. As you pass along the coast, there are, at intervals, citadels perched on the craggy bluffs above the sea like grey watch birds, each within eyesight of the other. As history tells it, if a Saracen ship was sighted approaching the coastline, the nearest tower would signal its neighbor in eyesight and I am told that by this means the whole coast could be alerted in one hour.

The entrance to Bonafaccio is dramatic—an opening in the cliffs which leads to a landlocked harbor, completely defensible. The old citadel sits on top of the cliff, still inhabited, where your nose leads you down and up the tangled alleys to the boulangerie with its five hundred year-old brick ovens. This is not a museum, it is a living town, and therefore the impact on the visitor is far greater. This is the land of Napoleon—it is poor and rocky and windy and feisty—a perfect breeding ground for a Bonaparte. The word 'food' seems much more appropriate here than 'cuisine'; the cooking is rugged like its people, and the wine reflects its birthplace in the mountain soil. Seafood is plentiful and good.

By nightfall the little harbor is filled with yachts. Dinner is taken at a restaurant on the quay presided over by a Madam perfectly cast in blue chiffon with rouged cheeks and apple-red lips.

Two Purees

The recipe below is a winter delight with roast meats and game and replaces potatoes or rice in the menu. Carrots are a complimentary color, taste and texture, to serve along with lentils.

Lentil Puree

Ingredients:

3 cups of quick-cooking lentils

1 tablespoon salt

1 peeled onion stuck with 2 cloves

1 bay leaf

1 stick (¼ cup) of melted butter

¼ teaspoon mace

¼ teaspoon ginger

½ cup of heavy cream

Cover the lentils with water. Add the salt, onion and bay leaf and bring to a boil. Lower the heat to a simmer and cook until the lentils are tender. Drain and remove the bay leaf and onion. Puree the lentils in a food processor, and add the remaining ingredients. Taste for salt and serve very hot. This dish can be made ahead and reheated slowly or in the oven.

Pouti

This recipe is from *The Cuisine of the Rose* by Murielle Johnston. As I have mentioned before, it is the definitive book on the cooking of Burgundy and Lyons and has been presented with great style by Random House. The pen and ink illustrations by Milton Glaser are especially fine.

Ingredients (serves 8):

9 potatoes, unpeeled

2 cans of chestnut Puree

Salt

Freshly ground black pepper

1 ½ cups milk (or white wine) preferably warm

Cook the potatoes in salted water. Peel the potatoes while they are still hot, holding them with a mitt or towel. Puree the potatoes in a food processor and add the chestnut Puree along with the milk until the mixture is light and fluffy. Season to taste.

Dressing Up the Ready Made

The way to beat the time clock can be to improve what has been sitting on the shelf or in the freezer. There are endless inventions using a combination of canned soups and everyone has a favorite, so I will move on to other suggestions here.

Salad Dressings

Take a package of Good Seasons Salad Dressing mix and prepare according to the directions, but use a really green, first-pressing olive oil, a good herb vinegar and a generous addition of dry mustard. Add a strong crumbled blue cheese (or other) for a cheese dressing on spinach or watercress.

A package of this same dressing can be added to the cooking water for rice.

Add a piece of garlic to the vinegar bottle.

Tuna

If you want a can of tuna to taste more like chicken, place it in a colander under cold running water and wash thoroughly. Drain and pat dry with a paper towel and voila! (Chicken of the sea).

Frozen French Fries

Maybe French fries are not in fashion but good ones are unbeatable with steak. Buy the frozen French fries in whatever cut preferred and fry them in hot vegetable oil until they just barely start to color, then remove to paper toweling. This can be done ahead of time. Just before serving, put them back in the reheated oil until they are the color you like, drain and serve. They will be crisp and delicious. It is the two steps that makes the difference.

A Very Good Lemon Meringue Pie

I know this will sound awful to the purist. But it is good even though the first ingredient is lemon Jell-O.

Use 1 package of the Jell-O lemon filling mix, adding a little real lemon juice if you like, but be sure to use 3 egg whites for the meringue.

Beat the egg whites and then add a nice amount of marshmallow fluff, folding it in gently.

Drop the meringue by large spoonfuls onto the cooled lemon filling in a baked pie shell and sprinkle with ½ tablespoon of sugar.

Bake at 350°F for seven minutes and let cool.

I am now going to give you another recipe which makes use of marshmallows. I am not going to put them on the top of sweet potatoes but they do marvelous things to fudge.

Fudge

Ingredients:

2 cups sugar

1 cup milk

4 ounces semi-sweet chocolate—best quality

1 teaspoon vanilla

1 tablespoon butter

5 marshmallows

Place the sugar, milk and chocolate in a heavy saucepan and bring to a boil, stirring once. Continue to cook until the fudge forms a soft ball when dropped into cold water. Add the remaining ingredients and cook for five minutes more.

Pour the fudge into a greased pan and let cool before slicing in squares with a buttered knife.

The French at Table

I have been reading a book about eating in France by Rudolph Chelminski, the roving reporter for *Readers Digest* in France, entitled simply, *The French at Table.*

If you have ever wondered how restaurant critics can ply their trade without the terrible fear of arriving at a many-starred table without an appetite, Mr. Chelminski has the answer. These masters of the eating art take along with them tiny little pills called *Sulfarlems*. To put it bluntly, they excite the liver, which advances the flow of bile, aiding quick digestion. All this agony to help the great unfed to find two forks or three toques for dinner.

A Little Scene at the Troisgros in Roanne

The following quote is from the *Guide Kleber*, which was one time the *Michelin Guide's* biggest competitor and, like Michelin, was owned by a tire company. Michelin eventually bought the controlling interest in Kleber and phased it out, but Jean Didier went on and founded the prestigious *Bottin Gourmand* and is once again giving Michelin a run for its money.

"When the waiter, Michel, proposed the vast Troisgros cheese platter, Jean [Jean Didier of *Guide Kleber*] came forth with some more discourse, lightly brushed with naughtiness this time. 'Young man, he said, I'm drinking the Bonnes-Mares '73, so I will choose my cheese in consequence. I will take one goat cheese only, and not too young. Never two women in my bed at the same time, and never two cheeses on my plate.'"

Tips from Thibaut: Reflections on Style

The Americans and Germans, when they go camping, tend to live roughly. The British, on the other hand, correctly believe that the cultured person always equates his authority and his behavior as a civilized human being through careful attention to style. Not for nothing did the representative of the British crown on the northern frontier of India always don evening dress, even when dining alone night after night.

In one of those glorious asides to a brutal and endless war, it fell upon my lot in 1944 when Stalingrad was thought to be lost, to be sent to the Soviet frontier through Kashmir, Tibet, and the tongue of Afghanistan between China and Russia to see whether a supply route to the Soviet Union might be built through that wild and unexplored region. My companions: a British Wing Commander who had flown so many sorties over Britain as to become a danger to himself and his men, and two young Russian women married to French prisoners of the Germans and in India on sufferance. Our cover was a snow leopard hunt in the northern Himalayas, which I went to Srinagar, Kashmir, to organize with the dean of hunt expeditions in the region, an Englishman named Coburn.

The four of us departed on the hunt with 37 horses, 17 guides, cooks, bearers etc., led by a magnificent Sikh. Before dawn each morning one group of bearers left camp to prepare the next night's stop. When the four of us arrived, tired from a long day's journey through the mountains, we found a roaring fire, water on the boil, four tents raised, with cots on whose sheeted surfaces a change of clothing had been laid, canvas bathtubs, and our Sikh to greet us with a request as to whether each of us preferred a whiskey before the bath, with, or just before dinner. There we were: two Russian women who had been saved as infants through Siberia to Manchuria, a British hero of the Battle for Britain and an American on leave from guerilla wars in China, enjoying British "style" in an unknown mountain vastness.

—Thibaut de Saint Phalle

Letter # 21

WINTER, 1986

"There is a lovely road that runs from Ixopo into the hills. These hills are grass-covered and rolling and they are lovely beyond any singing of it."

"Because the white man has power, we want power, he said. But when a black man gets power, when he gets money, he is a great man if he is not corrupted. I have seen it often. He seeks power and money to put right what is wrong, and when he gets them, why, he enjoys the power and the money. Now he can gratify his lust. Now he can arrange ways to get the white man's liquor, he can speak to thousands and hear them clap their hands. Some of us think when we have power, we shall revenge ourselves on the white man who has had power, and because our desire is corrupt, we are corrupted, and the power has no heart in it. But most white men do not know this truth about power, and are afraid lest we get it."

Cry The Beloved Country
—Alan Paton, 1948

South Africa

South Africa, the rough cut diamond, is set in the tip of the African continent, the Dark Continent for the trading ships who rounded her storm-lashed capes on their way into the Indian Ocean and the riches of southeast Asia. South Africa is not dark, it is giant blue skies and heavens of brilliant stars at night, hot colored flowers cascading from trees, and walls set in the valleys of treeless mountain ranges inhabited by leopards and snakes and homely baboons. There are dusty mountain passes, six thousand feet high. Some were widened into roads in the 1940s by Italian prisoners of war brought from the battles of North Africa and Sicily. These former animal routes thread their way west from the coast to isolated green valleys where water runs.

Johannesburg sits on a six thousand-foot throne in the central plain where the Transvaal and the Orange Free State meet. The avenues are lined with jacaranda trees which blanket the city in lavender colors come November. And Soweto, the darling of the self righteous American press, is poor yes, is black yes, but hardly blacker or poorer and certainly cleaner than the ghettoes attached to many American cities. South Africa, by our standards, is broom clean and is peopled by handsome races from the fair English and the robust Afrikaner to the fine-boned Zulu with the color and patina of polished mahogany. South Africa has the immenseness of the American west and the familiar stories of pioneers in covered wagons, territorial wars and gold rushes.

Natal and the kingdom of Swaziland are perhaps the most varied and lovely lands in South Africa. Natal is the land of horse farms, rolling hills and the beautiful city of Durban on the Indian Ocean. This area is populated in great numbers by Indians, so good curries can be found here.

Mala Mala

The largest private game preserve in the Union of South Africa is Mala Mala on the Mozambique border. It is also bordered by the Kruger National Park. The preserve covers approximately one hundred square miles of bush country with a luxury camp that will accommodate fifty people. We arrived on a chartered cargo plane from Johannesburg at the Kruger Park airport and then traveled by Land Rover one hour into the bush to reach what can only be described as a green oasis of beautiful camps, round and white, with thatched roofs, two swimming pools and two bathrooms with six-foot tubs for each bedroom camp. This bush country or veldt was formerly nineteen cattle ranches which had not been successful because of the constant battle with lions.

Evening comes while following a leopard who is tracking an impala under an orange sky with a soft wind. We stopped when the sky filled with stars to take a cool vodka tonic brought along in a cooler strapped to the land rover. Our native tracker, who rides in the shotgun seat, quickly sautés impala tidbits on a stove that has been brought along and serves them with a hot, peppery sauce. Later we were to find the leopard having his meal of fresh killed impala. There are over fifty species of animals living in a natural state on the preserve, and in our first twenty-four hours we saw leopards, lions, cheetahs, rhinos, zebras, impalas, giraffes, and elephants. You can advance to within ten feet of the animals as long as you do not put any part of your body out of the vehicle. It alone has no scent.

Mala Mala Elephant Stew

Ingredients (serves 3800):

1 medium sized elephant

1 ton of salt

1 ton of pepper

500 bushels of potatoes

200 bushels of carrots

4000 sprigs parsley

2 small rabbits (optional)

1.   Cut elephant into bite sized chunks. This will take about two months.

2.   Cut vegetables into cubes (another two months).

3.   Place meat in pan and cover with 4547 liters of brown gravy.

4.   Simmer for four weeks. Shovel in salt and pepper to taste.

5.   When meat is tender, add vegetables (a steam shovel is good for this).

6. If more guests are expected, add the two rabbits. However this is not really recommended because very few people like hare in their stew.

African Cuisine

Eating in Africa is not generally memorable, but there is an effort underway by the young African chefs to change all that, and a lot of credit for increased momentum can be given to the Sun Hotel chain and their executive chef, Billy Gallagher. November is the beginning of the shellfish season, and there is no sweeter shellfish in the world than a fresh crayfish. The tail meat of the "Rock Lobster" when fresh, not frozen, is as tender and sweet as the claw meat of a Maine lobster. Much of the cuisine of South Africa is inherited from the one-pot meals of the covered wagons heading north from the Cape. There is extensive use of lamb and venison, almost always overcooked, but the vegetables are fresh and well prepared. As I have said before, it seems to follow that the more undeveloped the country, the better the bread. Rich countries tend to refine their flour until there is nothing left of texture or taste. South Africa serves wonderful coarse grainy breads and, of course, scones with thick honey.

Ostrich Anyone?

East of Cape Town there is a great plain, the Klein Karoo, and it is here that you find the ostrich farms. Many of these large farms were created by Jewish families leaving the eastern European countries in the early part of the 20th century. Just about all of an ostrich is marketable, from the feathers to the skin (the leg skin is especially attractive), and the meat from the thigh makes a delicious stew. At a barbecue on one such farm we were treated to grilled ostrich preceded by scrambled ostrich eggs (a bit strong) served in half an egg shell which is the size of a soup bowl. The best thing of all, however, was an ostrich liver paté.

The Mount Nelson

Cape Town is primarily beautiful because of where it is situated. The coastline that rims it is truly awesome, but it is worth a trip there just to stay at the Mount Nelson. Here is one of the great old English colonial style hotels with bedrooms the size of ballrooms, generous covered porches, lovely gardens surrounding a swimming pool and old world service. It is painted sort of a Bermuda pink with white trim and has a great and beautiful lobby busy with faces from many lands. There you will find afternoon tea, ladies' bridge and eastern traders making their deals. Cape

Town, where the warm Indian Ocean meets the cold Atlantic, the people from both these oceans come together.

The Blue Train

The Blue Train, one of the great train trips left in the world, runs with slow majesty up through the Great Karoo of central South Africa, through the arid cattle country to Johannesburg. The train is royal blue with a cream stripe, whence it gets its name. Traveling at about fifty miles per hour the trip takes twenty-four hours. The accommodations are excellent as well as the service and food. It is a romantic adventure, in part because it is so unrushed.

Tips from Thibaut: South African Wine

One of the great political mistakes of all time was the revocation of the Edict of Nantes by Louis XIV and the consequent expulsion of the Huguenots from France. They founded Berlin and brought banking to Geneva and wine making to South Africa. The Huguenots settled in the beautiful valleys around Stellenbosch in the vicinity of Cape Town, facing west to get the moisture from the Atlantic and yet be safe from the southeastern Atlantic storms. Here are found the great wines of South Africa. Among the best are the following:

Chardonnays:
Hamilton Russell Vineyards
Backsberg

Burgundy:
Hamilton Russell Vineyards, Grand Van Noir
Meerlust Pinot Noir

Bordeaux:
Meerlust Rubicon
Delheim, Grand Reserve
La Boneur, Cabernet Sauvignon
Rustenberg, Cabernet Sauvignon

Whites:
Nederberg Steen Noble Harvest
Nederberg Weissir Riesling
Noble Late Harvest

These last two are *not* Chateau quem but for the price are splendid, semi-sweet dessert wines, worthy of any great cellar.
—Thibaut de Saint Phalle

In March of 1988 South Africa hosted the World Association of Cook's Societies.

> "We don't go to endorse the politics of those countries. We go to strengthen friendships and to share knowledge." And from the *Sun Magazine,* "Evidently we have a great deal to learn from these people. Not least a certain honest humility. They insist upon calling themselves cooks, though among them are some of the most outstanding and talented chefs in the world."

In the view of this writer the above attitude has a far greater and more positive influence on the friend in trouble than have sanctions, which are a negative, unproductive action.

Letter # 22

WINTER, 1987

New Year's Day, 1987, brings a northeasterly sashaying across the coastal marshes and villages of Virginia, blowing the old year away and making a clean sweep of last year's promises. The birds have flown to playing fields further south, leaving just gulls to keep things neat and tidy. So we set our thoughts in motion, racing across our minds like wind clouds. Time now to sketch out the year, mat it with humor, frame it in optimism, and hang it on our memory wall where it will most likely be ignored.

Winter Baking

The batter for the following muffins can be stored in a covered container in the refrigerator for up to six weeks. Twenty minutes before serving, either a single muffin in a custard cup, or more in tins, can be baked in a preheated oven for a fresh delight.

Six Weeks Bran Muffins

Ingredients:

1 cup boiling water

2 ½ teaspoons baking soda

½ cup shortening

1 cup sugar

2 eggs

2 ½ cups flour

2 cups All Bran

1 cup bran flakes

1 package chopped dates (optional)

1 cup chopped nuts

1 pint buttermilk

½ teaspoon salt

2 teaspoons baking powder

In a large bowl pour boiling water over the soda and let it cool. In another bowl cream the shortening, the sugar and the eggs. Add along with the remaining ingredients to the water mixture. Fill greased muffin tins three-quarters full and bake for about twenty minutes in a preheated 400°F oven.

Grandmother's Bread

This is my favorite white bread recipe and comes from James Beard. It is very reliable. Scald 2 cups of milk and pour into a large bowl. Add 1 tablespoon of butter and 1 teaspoon of salt. Cool the milk until it is warm on the wrist. In a measuring cup, dissolve one package of yeast in ¼ cup of warm water and sprinkle 1 teaspoon of sugar (or honey) over the top. As soon as the mixture starts to bubble, add it to the milk. Sift in 2 cups of flour (unbleached is better) and stir until the batter is smooth. Gradually stir in 3 more cups of flour or enough to make the dough stiff enough to handle. For whole wheat bread substitute 3 cups of wheat flour for 3 cups of white.

Turn out the dough on a lightly floured board and place a little extra mound of flour in the corner for further flouring of the hands and board, if necessary. Knead the dough until it is smooth and elastic and then place it in a clean bowl, cover with a kitchen towel and put out of drafts to let it double in bulk.

Now turn out onto the flour board again and knead for another five minutes. Divide it in half and shape into two loaves and place in oiled bread pans. Let the dough double in size again and then place the loaves in a preheated 400°F oven for forty-five minutes or until they pull away from the sides of the pans. Turn them out onto a rack for cooling. These loaves freeze very well after cooling.

Odds and Ends

The following recipes are simple on ingredients with a little surprise thrown in.

Escargots

Ingredients (serves 4):

8 ounces of garlic, minced

2 sticks of softened salted butter

Salt and pepper to taste

8 ounces of parsley

8 ounces of almond powder

48 escargots, canned

Preheat oven to 400°F.

Combine the first four ingredients and then add the almond powder. Place the snails in whatever you prefer, a small casserole, mushroom caps, or shells. Cover the escargots with the butter mixture and bake at 325°F for about seven minutes or until the butter is melted and bubbling.

Fish Cakes

Ingredients:

2 parts leftover salmon or swordfish

1 part mashed or boiled potatoes

1 egg

Salt and pepper and dill to taste

Combine the ingredients thoroughly with your hands and form into cakes or balls. Roll them in bread crumbs or corn meal and sauté in butter.

Pasta Sauce with Ricotta Cheese

Ricotta cheese can be combined with either some goat or Saga cheese and then thinned with whole milk to the right consistency.

Leg of Lamb

Marinate a leg of lamb for two days in red wine and then roast it in the marinade, adding to the pan some juniper berries, and cloves, whole garlic cloves and celery juice.

Tips from Thibaut: An Unusual Christmas Present

There is nothing more fun than starting one's own wine cellar. When I was young, I learned about French wines so that sommeliers in French restaurants would not, by their arrogant manner, indicate to my date that I knew nothing. Then one day I was asked by *Bride's Magazine* to write an article on starting a wine cellar for one hundred dollars. Believe it or not, I started with twenty different wines from lesser known but equally good estates and chateaux. This was in answer to Lichine's article in the *New York Times Magazine* saying you could start your own cellar with only two thousand dollars. I have been collecting wines ever since. This winter the thought occurred to us to start our married children down the same expensive highway. This is how I did it.

I took from my cellar twelve assorted French wines, some good, some excellent. I tried to include in the assortment the great wine areas like Bordeaux and Burgundy and also some of the lesser known regions like Chateau Neuf du Pape, Fronsac, and the Loire Valley. I mixed well known and lesser known but excellent vineyards. All were reds except one, because you don't find the same quality differences in white wine; just stay with the Burgundies, Mersault, Montrachet, Chablis, Macon and the like. I accompanied the wine with two marvelous books: the *Hachette Encyclopedia of French Wines* and a *Michelin* of wines with historical backgrounds, labeled explanations, maps and recommended vintages for both well known and unusual regions, including my cherished Gaillac. I also included an album for wine labels with space for comments and ratings. Each of my sons and sons-in-law received a memo from me identifying each wine and why I had chosen it.

—Thibaut de Saint Phalle

The Winter Side of the Summer House

Have you ever thought of the winter life of the summer house when it closes its doors and shutters against the outside world and lives within its walls? When it is no longer warm and friendly, when it no longer invites you in to stay? I returned one year in the winter and found that for nine months my gay, charming old fashioned friend led a solitary life with only the weather to rattle the doorknob.

It was late in February, when the lakes of northern Maine are thick with ice and snow which camouflages places, that I strapped on snowshoes and started across the lake to where my lovely island stood. Four little bundled up children followed in my wake, making us look like a mother duck and her brood. Conversation seemed out of place in the cold silence that comes with sub-zero air. There was no dock to climb up on and no steps up the hill to the lawn; only quiet came to greet us, having moved in while we were not there, in the camps, on the porch, by the well and the woodpile. The snow had taken away paths and steps and stumps and bushes. Every last detail was shrouded in a snow blanket just as though a Victorian housekeeper had scurried around after the family left, covering everything with white sheets. It seemed as though the island where we lived was like a lover in summer; once the lover was gone it took off its makeup and put away its party clothes. Gone were the bouquets of red geraniums that complimented the facades and where were the blue and white checked curtains that made the window laugh?

We left, we fair weather friends, and snowshoed quietly back across the lake to our other life.

tLW

Letter # 23

LATE WINTER, 1987

Washington is quiet this season, partly for diplomatic reasons. We are in a "lame duck" presidency and so there is a slow down, a let's wait and see attitude, which is just fine because the city has been brought to its knees, not with scandal, but with snow.

Floraculture

The demand for cut flowers and house plants is expected to double in the next fifteen years and, as a result, has become a very attractive alternative to agriculture in many tropical countries. Most of these countries are third world countries where labor is cheap and requires little land to turn a profit. In fact, when I was in South Africa, I saw fields of amaryllis blooming before being taken up and shipped to Holland, where they become Dutch bulbs, eventually sent to customers around the world. Columbia is the largest exporter of flowers after Holland and Britain; Spain and the United States are the smallest consumers per capita. The cold, long-wintered countries such as Sweden, Norway, and Switzerland are big importers of flowers and plants. The top ten cut flowers according to the Flower Council of Holland are, in order; rose, chrysanthemum, carnation, tulip, freesia, gerbera, lily, cymbidium, gypsophila and iris.

A Marinade for Venison

The following marinade was found in a book in which Raymond R. Camp describes how some of the game was prepared during a ten-day shoot at the hunting lodge of Alfred Krupp in the Austrian Alps. It is a superb marinade.

Ingredients:

8-10 pounds venison filet (or equivalent)

1 pint of dry red wine

1 wine glass of Calvados (or applejack)

4 peppercorns

1 tablespoon Tarragon

2 cloves of garlic

2 bay leaves

1 tablespoon salt

1 level teaspoon of freshly ground black pepper

With an ice pick or thin knife insert slivers of the garlic into the meat. Put the remaining ingredients into an earthenware container along with the meat and store in a cool place, not the refrigerator, for twenty-four hours. Turn the meat every so often.

Roast Venison

If you marinated a whole piece of meat, remove it from the marinade, reserving the marinade, and place it on slices of salt pork. Roast the meat at 450°F until it is just pink and transfer it to a warm platter. Pour off most of the drippings and then add 1 cup of strained marinade and a wine glass of Calvados and stir briskly while gradually adding 2 cups of sour cream. Serve with the thinly sliced venison.

Venison en Casserole

Now if you have marinated chunks of venison remove them from the marinade and dry them with paper toweling. In a brown paper bag place ½ cup of flour along with some salt and pepper and shake the meat, a few pieces at a time until they are lightly covered, then brown them in butter in a casserole. Pour strained marinade over them, cover and cook slowly until tender. Before serving, add a wine glass of Calvados and some sour cream and bring the sauce just to a simmer. Wild rice and red cabbage are the right things to serve with the venison, or puree of chestnuts can replace the cabbage. An apple dessert follows beautifully in its wake.

The marinade for venison will also do great things for lamb.

What's New

Trendy writers are telling us that Cajun cooking is done over dying embers, and restaurants are not only returning to French names but are quickly redecorating themselves into *bistros*. There is even a book by Irena Chalmers and friends called *American Bistros*, which tends to stretch the category a bit.

Best New Idea Department: pay less if you eat less. Some smart restaurants are experimenting with something the customer has wanted all along, and that is to have the option of ordering a smaller portion for a smaller price, especially at lunch. I have been tempted by the children's menu on occasion simply because it gave less food.

Time Magazine's Depressing Taste Test conducted by Korbel champagne of California. The purpose of the exercise was to determine what foods best complimented their champagne. This was a blind tasting using ten trained taste testers (I wonder where you train.) The results are surprisingly tasteless.

Prefered fried fish sticks to caviar and Oreos to strawberries

Taco filling over foie gras

Oriental pepper steak over escargots

Kentucky fried chicken over duck à l'orange

(Maybe the problem was the champagne)

Burgundy: The Heartland of France

Burgundy is an old place, maybe twenty thousand years older than the coming of Christianity. Because of its place on the map, trading routes crossed it, so it flourished long before Caesar arrived with his armies to conquer the Gauls in what was then Alesia. The Romans came with their wines and olives and ceramics, and when the Burgundians, big, strong, energetic, drinking Scandinavians, came a-conquering, they in turn were conquered by the growing of wine, the taming of the forests and the turning of the soil. Later, in the fifteenth century, the dukedoms, with robust figures and hearty names like Phillip the Bold and John the Fearless, galloped their horses across the land and filled their courts with high fashion and cuisine. What goes into the pot? Well, garlic and parsley were brought back from Egypt, sugar and spices from the Crusades to the Orient, and the Gauls loved to throw in a little pork.

The Burgundian cuisine is full of winter dishes, the fullest soups, the root vegetable, sausages and onions and generously shaped bottles of ruby red wine. This is not "nouvelle cuisine" but one of the oldest cuisines of civilization which has only improved with age, like the wines from its soil.

Puree de Choux

What could be so simple and yet unusual and perfect with pork?

Ingredients (serves 4):

1 head of cabbage quartered with the core removed

1 tablespoon of sweet butter

Salt and freshly ground pepper

Cook the cabbage in a pot of boiling salted water until soft and drain well. Process in a food processor, with the butter and seasoning, until smooth and serve warm.

Laitue Bourguignonne

We have the Romans to thank for introducing the salad. This warm one is for serving as a first course or as a bridge to later courses.

Ingredients (serves 8):

3 tablespoons of sweet butter

1 garlic clove peeled and crushed

Salt

Juice of a lemon

Freshly ground pepper

3 tablespoons minced parsley

Tender lettuce such as Bibb or Boston

Wash and dry the lettuce leaves thoroughly and place them in a glass or china bowl. Melt the butter slowly so that it is just warm, and then add the seasonings. Toss the salad with the dressing and serve immediately.

Côtes de Porc Farcies

Ingredients (serves 8):

8 slices finely chopped country or boiled ham

1 ½ cups graded or shredded Swiss cheese

3 teaspoons sage

Freshly ground black pepper

8 large, thick pork chops

3 tablespoons flour

4 tablespoons vegetable oil or lard

Salt

2 whole garlic cloves peeled

The first four ingredients are to be mixed to form the stuffing. Trim the chops well and with a sharp knife make a slit in each chop going all the way to the bone. Fill the pockets with the stuffing and secure with a tooth pick. Dredge the chops with flour, then brown them in the oil in a heavy skillet. Lower the heat, add salt and the garlic cloves, then cover and cook very slowly for about forty minutes. Serve the chops accompanied with the cabbage puree but with the addition of three potatoes which have been quartered and added to the boiling water with the cabbage and then processed with it.

Digestifs

There is nothing so pleasant at the end of a meal as to have something to soothe, a digestif, an eau de vie. They are not to be confused which are distilled from grapes only. The most notable coming from Cognac and Armagnac.

Liqueurs are composed of sugar, syrup, fruit and distilled alcohol and are therefore, very sweet.

'Eau de vie', meaning "waters of life" are made from alcohol and fruit so they stay dry and fresh. They usually follow a sweet desert. The best ones come from Alsace in France, Switzerland and Germany.

Kirsch—from Germany cherries and pits, also known as Kirshwasser.

Mirabelle—from yellow plums

Framboise—from raspberries

Fraise—from strawberries

Quetsch—from Alsatian plums

Letter # 24

EARLY SPRING, 1987

Time magazine, in its January 26th, 1987 issue, published an interview with M.F.K. Fisher by Mimi Sheraton, food critic. Miss Sheraton sensitively sketches impressions of her meeting with this wonderfully literate writer who happens to like to write about food. The interview points up the fact that to many her subject matter is beneath her literary talents, and to this she replies, "There is a communion of more than our bodies when bread is broken and wine is drunk. And that is my answer when people ask me: 'why do you write about hunger, and not wars or love?'"

If you have never read one of M.F.K. Fisher's books, just look at the array of appetizing titles: *Serve it Forth* (her first), *Consider the Oyster, How to Cook a Wolf.* The article begins with the introduction to her first book fifty years ago: "Now I am going to write a book. It will be about eating and about what to eat and about people who eat. And I shall do gymnastics by trying to not fall between these three fires, or by straddling them all . . . I set it forth."

The frequent mistake is isolating the subject of food from the world around it when in fact influence comes from the location, from the partakers, by the weather, by the time of the year or day, and certainly by the taste of the planner and the cook. Do you not remember a dinner taken in a room, or a salad set on a cloth on a table under the shade tree?—Well those moments are there, waiting like adjectives to bring life to the telling of a recipe, to help the reader sense the compatibility of the salad with the cloth and the cooling shade.

To quote from Peri Wolfman, owner of Wolfman, Gold & Good Company in New York, in her very interesting book, *Perfect Setting*:

"Setting the table is as important as cooking the food. Of course food is important; without the food there would be no meal. But there are simple delicious foods one can buy which require little in the way of preparation or cooking skills: cheeses and pâtés, crudities, and other infinite choices at a gourmet shop. But once the table is set, so is the mood and attitude for the experience . . . It is in the mood and spirit of these hectic times to set a beautiful table every night based on the simple, the doable, and the affordable."

Some Fine Ideas

Use an ice cream or melon scoop to make balls out of soft butter. These can then be put on a butter plate for a formal dinner or pushed into a crock or jar for the table.

A rag rug as a picnic tablecloth looks stunning; they come in many sizes and colors and are machine washable. A pretty and inexpensive table covering is a quilted mattress pad used as the table skirt and blue and white tattersall linen kitchen towels set the long way as place mats. Large green leaves that lie flat, such as grape, make good basket liners, as do crisp bunches of curly parsley with the stems removed. Parsley looks beautiful in a shallow silver bowl for serving stuffed olives or cherry tomatoes.

It used to be traditional to give a beautiful teacup as an engagement present. The bride would end up with a very attractive collection of unmatched cups. This can also be done with coffee or demitasse cups and why not dessert plates? Brides are having a hard time coming up with a dozen Tiffany plates from one donor so there could be the alternative of a plate and cup shower in a specific color range. These gifts would certainly make an interesting table setting.

This is an ingenious table setting for a children's party: cover the table with heavy white vinyl, which can be bought by the yard, and write a big happy birthday on it with colored magic markers. Each child's name can be written by his place, if you like. Supermarket white terry face cloths become napkins. A helium-filled balloon is tied to each chair and food is served on colorful thick vinyl plates from the party store. Flat bottom mugs are better than cups and are a good investment when frequently entertaining children. For young children, cluster all candles at one end of the cake so that short puffs can put them out with ease.

Beef Italian Style

Italian cuisine is surely one of the finest in the world. It has the distinction of being sophisticated in taste and look without ever falling into the pit of pretension. When I think about the food of Italy, I visualize platters of reds and greens like blood red hams, red shrimps and tomatoes, all redder than anywhere else, big flat leaves of parsley, spinach-green noodles and green olive oil. Italian cooking is a riot of color, straightforward as a bunch of field flowers.

Carpaccio

Classic Italian carpaccio's simplicity derives from the quality of its ingredients.

Ingredients:

3 lemons

1 medium-size clove of garlic peeled but left whole

½ cup olive oil

Salt and freshly ground pepper

1 pound champignon mushrooms

8 thin slices of Parmigiano (about 2 ounces each)

8 very thin slices of top round beef

8 sprigs Italian parsley, leaves only.

First squeeze the lemons into a small bowl. Take a glass or crockery bowl, and holding the garlic with a fork, rub it well over the entire surface of the bowl. Add the oil in a slow stream while still rubbing the garlic around the bowl. Add the lemon juice in the same manner and then season with salt and pepper. Put the sauce aside. Wipe the mushrooms with a damp cloth and then slice them thinly and line them on the bottom of a crockery platter. Make an outer ring of the Parmigiano slices over the mushrooms. Lay the beef slices overlapping in the center of the platter and pour the reserved sauce over all. Decorate the platter with the parsley leaves.

This dish can also be artfully arranged on individual plates but the meat will only keep its bright color if it is kept waiting but a short time.

Melanzane al Forno (Baked Eggplant)

Ingredients (serves 6):

2 very large and round eggplants

4 tablespoons olive oil

4 cloves garlic, peeled and cut into six slivers each

Salt and freshly ground pepper

5 sprigs Italian parsley, leaves only

Preheat oven to 350°F.

Oil two baking dishes of about 13 ½ by 8 1/4 inches with 1 tablespoon of the oil for each. Wash the eggplant, remove the stems and slice into 1-inch thick rounds. Arrange the eggplant slices in one layer in the baking dishes and insert 2 slivers of garlic in each. Season with salt and pepper and drizzle the remaining oil over the eggplant. Bake for twenty-five minutes and transfer the slices to a serving platter or to individual plates and scatter the parsley leaves over them. Serve at once.

These above recipes were taken from Giuliano Bugialli's *Foods of Italy* (www.bugialli.com).

Gelato Spazzacamino

The combination of flavors and texture makes this simple dessert one of my favorites.

Ingredients:

1 or 2 scoops of rich vanilla ice cream

2 teaspoons of espresso, ground and then powdered in a blender (it also comes powdered in a jar)

1 to 2 tablespoons Scotch whiskey

Just before serving, place the ice cream in a shallow bowl or deep plate. Sprinkle the powdered espresso over the ice cream and pour the whiskey over it.

Linguine Con Le Noci

Ingredients:

1 pound linguini

Salt

¼ cups walnuts

1 clove garlic, slightly mashed

1 cup heavy cream

3 tablespoons butter cut into pieces

1 cup freshly grated parmesan cheese

Put the linguini into a large pot of boiling water and cook until done to your taste. While the linguini is cooking, place the walnuts and garlic in a food processor and run for fifteen or twenty seconds. Add the cream and process a few seconds more. Add 2 tablespoons of the cooking water and a little salt and process a couple of seconds. Remove the contents to a large bowl and add the cheese and the butter. When the linguini is done, drain it and add it to the sauce, toss well and serve.

Follow this pasta with a watercress salad with a dusting of freshly ground pepper.

Letters Home

Moving is in the same category as a day in a marble floored museum or an endless stand-up cocktail party where they have removed all the chairs. But in moving there is at least the reward of coming across old papers and letters left for years unread. I came across a letter which, because of its prominent garnet crest and subtitle, caught my eye: "Buckingham Palace." The letter was dated December 28, 1918 and was from my grandfather to my mother, then a student at Miss Porter's School in Farmington, Connecticut. It reads in part;

"Pussy Cat, Pussy Cat,

Where have you been?

I've been to London to visit the Queen.

And so have I.

I'm not sleeping in Buckingham Palace, but I dine here most every evening; and I must say that the Queen is a very good housekeeper; we have almost as good food as we have at home. It reminds me, in fact, of Mother's own Thursday night at home. And a very splendid gentleman in a red coat and plush smalls waits upon us just about as formally and formidably as a Bishop might.

I'm frightened to death of him, for I know if I forgot my table manners and ate with my knife or forgot to crook my little finger when I sipped my demitasse, he would order me out of the palace to be shot at dawn."

Scene two: one month earlier:

"Somewhere in France, November 18, 1918

Do you know where the "Somewhere in France" is? I am in the bomb proofs of Verdun Citadel. We went to Virton and there we found a hospital with four hundred wounded Germans in it. After the hospital we had a luncheon at a funny little inn where the German officers had lived till last night. Incidentally, they had gone away without paying the French woman who had kept them for four years. But she didn't seem to care as long as she was rid of them. And we had a fine dinner—first, a good soup—then roast meat, potatoes, cabbage, and tea. The meat was horsemeat, but we are all used to that over here; and the tea she told us had been buried in the back yard for four years. It tasted like it too, but we were too polite to say so; and when we paid her she made change in Belgian money that she had kept buried ever since the war began. I have the change in my pocket now. She also had buried all of her dining-room ornaments and these she brought out in our honor."

Two meals, a study in contrasts one might say, but not really. They were both the best that they could be and that is the pleasure in them.

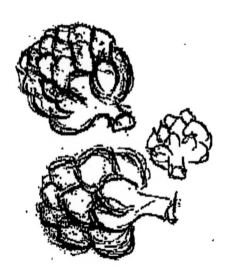

Letter # 25

LATE SPRING, 1987

The Embassy of Iraq is in one of the loveliest residential hideaways in Washington, occupying a symmetrical red brick Federal/ Colonial style house so popular now in this area. Inside, however, it is furnished in the faux French style of painted white with gold trim, a taste in decor that is ever popular with embassies. The ambassador is a young man who decorates his talks with historical notes, taking great pride in the fact that his country has a story covering six thousand years. The young age of the United States, he says, gives it flexibility which his country finds more difficult because of the great influence a long history has in its decisions. But old age has the advantage of experience.

The dinner was catered by Lebanese cooks because there are no Iraqi caterers in town and the Lebanese cuisine is very similar to their own. A whole side of roasted lamb waited on the buffet table. When carved, it was lovely and pink inside and aromatic with herbs. The breads were coarse and good and were accompanied by bowls of humus.

The only sad note in the evening was the photographs of dusty boy soldiers on tanks smiling out from silver frames among the knick-knacks on the tables.

Spring Time Desserts

Red, white and blue and right in season.

Strawberries with Blueberry Sauce
or
Blueberries with Raspberry Puree

Ingredients (serves 4):

1 ½ cup blueberries (or raspberries)

1 tablespoon superfine sugar

1 pint strawberries

1 cup whipped cream

The blueberry sauce must be made at the last minute so that it will not turn color. Place the berries and the sugar in the container of a blender and purees. Strain the puree into a bowl and then spoon some sauce onto each plate. Arrange the hulled strawberries in a circle in the sauce and put a dessert spoon of whipped cream in the center. If you use the raspberry sauce it can be made ahead as it does not discolor.

Strawberry Delight

Ingredients:

1 basket of the largest strawberries

Orange liqueur

You will need a plastic syringe with a large needle. Fill the syringe with orange liqueur and inject the needle close to the hull of the strawberry until it reaches the cavity. Gently release the liqueur filling into the cavity. Arrange the strawberries on plates either on one of the purees above or serve with pound cake or powdered sugar.

The recipe, as you can imagine, came from my doctor, who would cure all my problems with a session in the kitchen inventing new tasty treats instead of treatments.

Strawberries au Vin

A very simple way to serve strawberries, which is popular in France.

Ingredients:

1 quart of cleaned, whole strawberries of more or less equal size

3 tablespoons sugar

½ cup of a light red wine

In a bowl combine the strawberries with the sugar and then pour the red wine over. Chill for several hours before serving.

Away We Go!

We are off to the continent—as they used to say—in a few days, and I will be spending time with a couple of cooking schools to tell you about. We will also be eating mostly in the bistros because that is what we prefer, whether the dollar is up or down. There will be a little time spent in the great gastronomic city of Lyon and a little time in the city of Geneva. Food aside, the height of the hemline is the conversational interest of the moment and reminds me of Coco Chanel's remark "the most unattractive part of the body is the knee."

May is the month to make a shopping list of wines for summer drinking, so consider white wines, also a selection of Italian wines, which are as fresh as a morning dew and at as fair a price as any good wine around.

Peas in a Pod

Fresh young peas are on their way and there is hardly a vegetable that can compare. Remember when cooking green vegetables to add them slowly to the boiling water, as the drop in water temperature is what dulls their color. This method does not then require cooking with salted water. Also remember to shell the peas at the last minute before cooking, as they lose their sugar quickly.

Puree of Peas St. Germaine

Adapted from *The Escoffier Cook Book*

Place freshly shelled peas in a pot with a ½ teaspoon of salt and a pinch of sugar. Add a lettuce leaf tied together with a few sprigs of parsley and cover with boiling water. Cook until done and drain them, reserving the cooking liquid. Reduce the cooking liquid over high heat until it is almost all gone. Puree the peas in a processor or through a sieve, add a little fresh butter and then the reduced cooking liquid until it is the consistency you want.

Green Peas á la Menthe

Cook the peas in salted water along with a bunch of fresh mint tied with a string. Drain and add sweet butter and place in a serving dish with a sprig of fresh mint as garnish.

Fresh Pea Soup with Orange

From *Cook's Magazine*'s cookbook

Ingredients (serves 4):

3 cups chicken stock canned or fresh

4 cups shelled fresh peas (about 4 pounds)

Pinch of sugar

½ teaspoon of grated orange zest

¾ cup of heavy cream

Salt and black pepper

3 tablespoons heavy cream whipped (optional)

Bring the stock to a boil and add the peas and sugar and cook until tender. Strain the peas, reserving the stock and puree them in a blender or processor, then return them to the stock through a sieve. Add the orange zest, cream, salt and pepper. The soup may either be heated or chilled before serving and topped with a spoonful of whipped cream, sour cream or crème (fraîche).

Baby New Potatoes

So far we have desserts for spring and peas for spring and so now we have to prepare those sugar-sweet new potatoes.

Lemon-Dill Potatoes

Ingredients (serves 4):

12 baby new potatoes of equal size

3 tablespoons fresh lemon juice

4 tablespoons sweet butter

6 tablespoons fresh chopped dill

Peel the potatoes and boil them in lots of water until done but not soft. Drain the potatoes and pour over them 3 tablespoons of fresh lemon juice. Turn them carefully to coat them well and then drain off the juice. Add the butter and toss gently. Place the potatoes in a serving dish and sprinkle the dill over the top.

Potato and Truffle Salad

From *Chez Panisse Menu Cookbook*

Ingredients (serves 6):

12 red or white new potatoes (pick out the smallest ones you can find of uniform size)

1 tablespoon salt preferably sea salt

3 large shallots

¼ cup white wine vinegar

Black truffles

½ cup of extra virgin olive oil

Black pepper

Put the unpeeled potatoes in a pot and cover with water by an inch. Add the salt, cover and bring to a boil. Remove the cover and cook at a strong simmer for five to ten minutes, but keep checking the potatoes with a knife to be sure they do not become overdone.

While the potatoes are cooking, dice the shallots and put them in a small bowl covered with vinegar and salt.

When the potatoes are done draining, peel them if you prefer and then slice them and toss carefully with whatever amount of sliced truffles you can afford.

Slowly add the oil and pepper to the vinegar, then combine gently with the potatoes and let the salad rest awhile so that the truffles can do their work.

Whenever possible boil your potatoes in the skin and peel after. The taste and texture are noticeably better.

Letter # 26

LATE SPRING, 1987

Spring is finding its way into the valley of the Rhone even as the April snows stubbornly dust the mountains of the Alps. The great river runs from east to west where it is contained to form Lake Geneva. From time to time divers retrieve household articles from earlier civilizations that lived in the man made valley. Skiers cascade down from above the tree line of these hard-edged mountains, down to where the snow melts and the first wild flowers are appearing. These are young mountains. Old mountains are softly rounded, mellowed, sort of worn down like an old tooth, where younger mountains are razor edged and uncompromising. In the markets are the first white asparagus and strawberries of robust size and ruddy color.

The tourist life is an expensive one this year in Europe, but this fact has not stopped Americans from making summer reservations. It may be that it is not a decline in the dollar, but terrorism, that has influenced the traveler. On the part of many visitors though, there is genuine resistance to the price increases that have been made at the more expensive hotels and restaurants, and these are opting to give up a toque or a star for, in many cases, something just as fine but less expensive. The middle easterners with their large entourages have fled Paris for Greece, leaving several hotels, which had been arranged to service them in bankruptcy.

Pommes Frites or Fresh French Fries

Real French fries should be light and puffy and a little crisp and hot, not too thick or too thin nor tasting of grease, so here is the way to do them.

Slice good fresh dry Idaho potatoes into either shoestring, if you prefer, or about ¼-inch thick sticks and immediately drop into a bowl of ice water.

Heat fresh vegetable oil until hot but not smoking. While the oil is heating remove the potatoes from the water and dry on toweling. Drop them by handfuls into the fat, being careful to not crowd the pan, and cook them until they just begin to show color. Remove the potatoes to paper toweling to drain and continue in this manner until they are all done.

Before serving, drop the potatoes again into the reheated fat and cook until they are the color you prefer. Drain on a paper toweling and salt and serve immediately. They will keep warm folded inside a white napkin.

Pommes de Terre Soufflées or Fancier Fries

Now these are really beautiful!

Peel and trim Idaho potatoes into neat oval shapes and then cut them lengthwise into 1/8-inch slices or use a mandoline. Put them in the ice water for fifteen minutes minimum, then proceed with the first frying, as in the previous recipe, with the fat cooking at 275°F. If you are not going to finish them right away, store them in the refrigerator until later. Heat the oil to 400°F or until it is about to smoke, and fry in small batches until light brown and puffed up. Drain, salt, and serve immediately.

Mére Michel

Mere Michel is a twenty-five chair bistro in Paris. It is not on anyone's list, is cozy, family run and specializes in seafood, but is also known for its dessert omelets, which are beautiful and runny, shiny brown on top and follow seafood beautifully. There is a Grand Marnier and a devastating chocolate. You must cross an alley to get from the dining room to either the kitchen or the bathroom, which must present problems when it is necessary to carry the omelets in one hand and the umbrella in the other. Here is a recipe for omelette soufflée.

Omelette Soufflée

Ingredients:

1 ½ squares very fine chocolate, grated

5 ½ tablespoons sugar

4 large eggs

Preheat oven to 350-400°F.

Separate the eggs and beat the yokes, until they are very light, with 5 tablespoons of sugar. Stir in the grated chocolate. Beat the egg whites until stiff, adding ½ a tablespoon of sugar for the last few minutes, then fold them lightly but thoroughly into the yolks. Butter a heatproof serving platter and spread the mixture evenly on the platter with a spatula. Make a 2-inch crease down the middle of the omelet with the spatula and place in a 350-400°F oven for about twenty minutes, depending on how runny you want it. You can glaze the soufflé by sprinkling a little sugar over the surface for the last few minutes.

Good Ideas

Good ideas are usually simple ones, as for example the use in Europe of the tea cart as the "Silent Servant." What it means is that you too can be a part of the conversation at your own table. It is, after all, distracting to have the hostess in perpetual motion, so set the cart in the kitchen ahead of time with everything that will be needed for serving the courses not already on the table, plates and cutlery on the bottom and serving dishes on the top. When changing courses simply put the dirty plates on the bottom shelf and the clean ones on the table. If there is not enough room, the dessert plates and dessert can always be put on a sideboard, but the point is that you never have to leave the room. Wheel the cart to wherever you are serving the meal and join the party. If the cart needs to go out on the terrace, the bigger the wheels the better. If you build one, use children's bicycle wheels.

Here are some good ideas from a day at La Varenne Cooking School in Paris (www.lavarenne.com—more on the school next month), where young Americans are learning to be chefs and caterers and other Americans are learning for pleasure.

Folded damp kitchen towels are placed on top of simmering pots to keep the contents submerged (as in the case of artichokes which bob up like apples).

Round cake racks were used all the time to strain liquids from pots.

Monkfish was the preferred fish for making fish stocks.

A knife sharpener was kept close by for constant sharpening during preparation of dishes.

When chopping with a knife use *only* the thick end.

Good Recipes

Celery root makes an unusually good puree.

Soak bread for stuffing in a little cognac.

If you want your chicken skin crispy, rub it with salt before roasting.

Poach pears in cassis, then take the left over liquid and boil it down to syrup to make a sorbet.

Poach an orange in Grenadine to give the skin a lovely color, then julienne the skin for garnish.

Pears poached in wine can stay in their liquid for up to two weeks if covered.

Pears in Red Wine

Ingredients (serves 8):

8 firm pears

½ cup sugar

Strip of lemon zest

2-inch piece of cinnamon stick

2 ½ cups red wine

Few drops of lemon juice

Chantilly cream (¾ cup heavy cream whipped in a chilled bowl until it holds its shape with the addition of 2 teaspoons of vanilla).

In a saucepan just large enough to hold the pears standing up, place the sugar, lemon zest, cinnamon, lemon juice and wine and cook until the sugar is dissolved. Then boil for five minutes and let cool. Meanwhile peel the pears and core them carefully from the bottom, then take a small slice off the bottom so they stand up. Place them in the syrup and, if the wine does not cover them, add more. Cook them covered for twenty minutes, then keep testing them until they are done but not soft. Let them cool in their syrup.

Remove the pears from the liquid and stand them in a shallow bowl. Strain the syrup, then cook it down until it is thick. Adjust the lemon juice and add sugar if necessary. Cool slightly, then spoon over the pears and refrigerate. Cover if they are to hold overnight. Serve with a bowl of Chantilly cream.

P.S. Add 1 teaspoon of black or green peppercorns to the red wine with the cinnamon stick for Peppered Pears in Red Wine.

Spring Season at the Four Seasons

The Four Seasons Cookbook is a collection of recipes separated by season; it therefore focuses on fresh seasonal ingredients. It was published in 1971 by The Ridge Press with a forward by James Beard who was a consultant to the restaurant.

Puree of Pimentos

Ingredients (serves 6):

2 pounds fresh sweet red peppers

¼ cup vegetable oil

1 cup rice

4 cups water

Salt to taste

6 tablespoons of sweet butter

Remove the stems and seeds from the peppers and cut them up. Put the oil in an ovenproof casserole, add the peppers and bake in the oven for fifteen minutes at 400°F. Baste the peppers every five minutes with the oil. When they are done add the rice, water and salt and bake at 350°F for another thirty minutes. Place in a blender or food processor and add the butter last.

Serve this dish with chicken or meat.

Cream of Avocado Soup

Ingredients (serves 6):

1 large avocado

1 pint chicken stock

1 teaspoon chili powder

¼ teaspoon coriander

1 cup heavy cream

Red caviar

Peel and cut up the avocado and process in a blender or food processor until smooth, along with the chicken stock, coriander and chili powder. Pour into a double boiler and heat for ten minutes. Cool, then add the cream and chill thoroughly. When serving, decorate each serving with a teaspoon of red caviar.

Letter # 27

SUMMER, 1987

"Going to the country" is part of summer that has not changed a great deal except that there used to be marvelous trains that went out through the land to the old resort places, carrying all the people and things that now are packed into station wagons, which have replaced the train, rather than meeting it.

I first took the State of Maine Express with my mother when I was six weeks old. She put me in a wicker laundry basket and hung it with two cords from the upper berth where I swung my way down to Maine on a late June night. Portland, Maine, was an important station in the era of trains since trains were changed there for places like Poland Springs or Kennebago Lake, and the Bar Harbor Express revived itself for the run up the coast. The most important and prosperous man at the Union Station was Eddie Cummings, because he was not only the head redcap but also owned every concession in the station. When you got off the train in the early morning, you would have breakfast in Eddie's diner, read Eddie's newspaper and supply the children with candy from his machines, while he transferred the luggage and walked all the dogs that had spent the night in the baggage car. My grandmother and later my mother would write Eddie at the station in the beginning of spring to tell him what train we would be on and how many children and dogs had to be cared for and fed, and he would be waiting on the platform to greet us and all his other friends.

Many years later, when he was old and very well off and a legend to those who went down to Maine by train, my mother asked him to come have supper with us in Falmouth Foreside, and we cooked chicken on the grill and listened to "Going to Maine for the Summer," stories of the rich and famous in Maine.

Going to the Country with Moveable Menus

Take to the country what is best from where you live. What first comes to mind is meat. Small towns often do not have a butcher, and the supermarket is not likely to have fresh lamb or veal very often. Have the butcher prepare, wrap and mark the cuts you want, freeze and pack them in a box with dry ice for the journey.

They will keep frozen for a long time.

If you are interested in precooking some weekend meals to take away with you, how they are packed for the trip can be the difference between airline quality and delicious. Undercooking is many times advisable, as you will be reheating. Carry the meats and fish in separate containers from their juices or sauces. This gives you more serving options, especially if you want to serve the food cold at some point. Purees are wonderful travelers. Add the cream when reheating.

Bake the cake but take the icing separately; it is much easier to transport.

A tip from the Raynors' article in *Vogue* is to make your sherbet and take it out of the freezer just before leaving. It will thaw on the way, but just refreeze it in individual servings. Do not touch a box of berries until meal time or they will not last.

Make up good cookie dough for your hostess and take it with you from your freezer along with a baking sheet.

Take with you a bottle of chilled white wine, a handmade Bloody Mary mix in one container and a fresh fruit mix for rum punch in another for the evening's view from the porch rocker just before dusk.

Remember that there are many places in this land that only sell iceberg lettuce and spongy bread. Wrap the lettuce in damp towels, then put it in plastic bags for the trip.

Mariana's Clam and Chicken Pie

Cruising with Newbold Lawrence was always a gastronomic experience as he was a natural cook, an inventor of many great dishes from ordinary ingredients. At sea he was a genius, a former submarine man from the Academy and, at the time of this story, was running the operations department of United States Lines. His cooking and his garden were heavily influenced by his years in France and the Orient.

On one choppy day we left the end of Long Island, and headed east aboard his big comfortable wooden ketch. The motion below deck was unsettling, but Newbold decided to light the huge black iron monster of a stove on which he cooked in the forward part of the cabin. He called me to help in the galley, and it is still in my memory: the heat, the motion, the smell of the food and its effect on a very pregnant sous-chef. But the dinner was superb. The following pie was served up that evening in a starry lighted cockpit with a soft southwester blowing our cares away. Clam pies have been around a long time but the addition of chicken makes very good company.

Ingredients (serves 6):

3 pounds clams in shells, scrubbed, or a pint of shelled fresh oysters that are sold in jars

2 chicken breasts, boned and simmered in water for fifteen minutes (reserve the water)

4 tablespoons butter

½ cup sliced mushrooms (optional)

2 tablespoons chopped onions

¼ cup flour

¼ teaspoon salt

1 cup half and half

1 tablespoon lemon juice

2 tablespoons chopped parsley

A little Worcestershire sauce

A jigger of sherry

Salt and pepper to taste

Dough for a 9-inch pie crust

If you are using clams, place them in a pot with a little water and bring to a boil. Turn the heat down and simmer until the shells open, stirring occasionally. Drain and reserve the liquid. If the clams are large, they can be cut in half. If you are using the oysters, bring them to a simmer and drain them, reserving the liquid.

Melt butter in a skillet; add the onions and the mushrooms and sauté until tender. Off the heat, stir in the flour and salt, then 1 cup of clam or oyster juice. Return the pan to low heat and stir a minute or two before adding the half and half in a steady stream while stirring. Add the remaining ingredients and cook until the sauce has thickened a bit. More juice can be added if it becomes too thick.

Add the clams or oysters and pour the mixture into a deep dish, then cover with the pie crust, crimping the edges to hold the liquid. Make a few air holes.

Brush the top with a beaten egg and bake at 350°F for twenty-five minutes or until the crust is a nice color.

Odds and Ends

Fresh Peach Sauce

In the container of a blender put 1 cup of peeled, sliced peaches and the same of softened vanilla ice cream. Add ¼ cup of rum, cover and run until smooth. Serve over fresh fruit (from *Gourmet Magazine*, April 1962).

Amaretti

Ingredients:

12 ounces of almonds

1 cup of sugar

½ teaspoon almond extract

2 egg whites

Pulverize the almonds in a food processor and then add half the sugar and the almond extract.

In a separate bowl, beat the egg whites until they form soft peaks.

Add the remaining sugar and beat until stiff peaks are formed.

Combine the two mixtures thoroughly but gently.

Shape into balls of 2-inch diameter and place on a greased cookie sheet 1 inch apart.

Bake at 350°F for about five minutes or until they are light brown.

Avocado with Prosciutto

Ingredients (serves 2):

1 small avocado peeled and sliced lengthwise into thin strips

Moisten the slices with 2 teaspoons of fresh lime juice and arrange them fan shaped on two plates.

Drape 2 ounces of prosciutto over the avocados and serve.

Sour Sweet Chocolate Cake

I believe that this recipe for chocolate cake is one of the easiest and best you will come across.

To start with:

Cream

½ cup shortening

1 ¼ cups sugar

Add:

3 eggs

Melt:

4 ounces chocolate

Add 2 heaping teaspoons instant coffee

1 cup water

Mix:

½ cup flour

1 teaspoon baking powder

1 teaspoon baking soda

Add alternately with chocolate to sugar mixture.

Bake thirty to forty minutes at 350°F.

Vacation Cooks

If you are going to a rental vacation house, remember to take:

A cook book

A portable grill

Two good knives

A good cork screw

A pepper mill

The best olive oil

A heavy bottomed sauté pan

An apron

Birthday Book

For my birthday I received a new cookbook entitled *Cooking in the Nude: Playful Gourmets,* by Debbie Cornwell. It was published in a place called Citrus Heights, California (of course).

The chapter titles are: Cheap Frills (Creating the mood); Does Size Really Matter (presentation); Before Play (pantry needs); Appeteasers; Lettuce Be Lovers (salads); Piece De No Resistance (entrées); Something on the Side (vegetables); Index; Naughty Notes.

There are delightful image-provocative recipe titles such as: Carnal Coq Au Vin, Birds in Bondage, Simmering Denouement and Getting Hot Chops.

Oddly enough, however, they have omitted the dessert course. Maybe it comes later.

A Little White Lie

I promised that I would present some light picnic wines from Italy, and I have tasted away but have yet to put one word on their behalf on the blank white pages. I had to say something because I said I would. I even asked my husband if he would write about Italian white wines for me, but to no avail (his "Frenchness" reared its Gallic nose). But I have been saved, and by the dear old *New York Times* magazine and an article by Frank Prial called "True Confession." He claims that he was prompted to confess because in today's news climate you can get easily published if you are willing to confess something. So we have a literary cleansing of this man who dares to admit that he does *not* like white wine, with a few great exceptions, especially those coming out of Italy and Spain. He dares to say that "white is to wine what American Colonial is to furniture. "No one expects white wine to taste like anything and it almost never does. White wine is a time filler, something to do with your hands," and on he goes. "There are, of course, the glorious exceptions from that little part of Burgundy where one finds the Montrachet and Meursault, but they are dearly priced, so we turn to the ordinary-income wines of Macon, Chablis and Muscadet, not to forget the Sancerres. Italy has the whites from Alto Adige and the Gravi from Piedmont."

I agree with Mr. Prial when he says that California whites tend to be a lot like, but never as good as, the Loire Valley. When in doubt, order a red wine anywhere in the world, as it will almost always be better than white wine. So go chill a nice light Beaujolais on a hot day, smell its bouquet, taste its character on your palate and enjoy what it does for *your* character. Don't forget that good white is harder to make than red and every so often you may be lucky enough to meet a lovely light refreshing blond, well bottled with a fine body, but it will most likely not be at the cocktail bar, where "just a glass of white wine, please" will just introduce you to another "vin ordinaire."

Letter # 28

SPRING, 2004

Since it is the beginning of spring, I am reminded of the blue crabs about to shell along the Virginia coast and how we floured them, then sautéed them in some butter and garlic until just golden, removing them to plates and place them on toast squares. I then scraped the pan clean with a little white wine, poured it over the crabs and sprinkled them with chopped parsley. We would take our plates out on the porch, along with the rest of the bottle of wine, and with the salty, damp and hazy summer southerly puffing up the estuaries we ate our meal, trying to talk above the daily chatter of the very vocal and immensely varied sea birds in the great salt marshes of the Virginia barrier islands.

Avocado Crab Cakes

Here is an excellent recipe for crab (or salmon) cakes.

Ingredients (serves 4):

1 avocado

1 lemon

1 teaspoon chopped chives

1 teaspoon chopped dill

1 egg lightly beaten

2 tablespoons mayonnaise

1 tablespoons Dijon mustard

¼ cup dry bread crumbs

1 pound fresh back fin crabmeat

¼ cup olive oil

Salt and pepper

Peel and chop the avocado, put it in a bowl and moisten the avocado with the juice from half a lemon.

Chop the chives and dill, place in another bowl and combine, along with the egg, mayonnaise and mustard. Add half the bread crumbs then the crab meat, and mix with your hands until just blended. Form the crab mixture into eight cakes and roll in the remaining half cup of bread crumbs.

Heat 2 tablespoons of olive oil and cook the cakes over medium heat until heated through and a nice golden color. Serve with lemon wedges.

Salmon or Tuna Fish Cakes

Ingredients:

½ pound cooked salmon or tuna

1 tablespoon each chopped fresh chives and tarragon

1 teaspoon each minced garlic and crushed green peppercorns

1 tablespoon each Dijon mustard and mayonnaise

1 teaspoon fresh lemon juice

2 tablespoons olive oil

Combine all the ingredients in a bowl and season to taste. With floured hands, form the mixture into four to six cakes and store in the refrigerator until ready to cook.

Prepare a second mixture using a different fish. Brown the cakes in one or two skillets using olive oil and serve the cakes on a bed of either the fresh tomato or sorrel sauce.

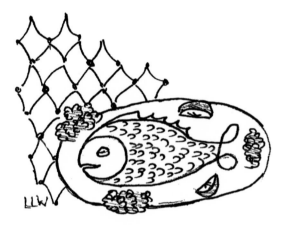

Sorrel Sauce for Fish Cakes

This recipe for sorrel sauce comes from Richard Wilbur who wrote *The School for Wives* and received the Pulitzer Prize in 1957.

Ingredients:

2 cups cream

⅛ cup lemon juice

1 ½ tablespoons green peppercorn mustard

⅛ teaspoon nutmeg and salt and pepper to taste

1 tablespoon unsalted butter

Heat the above ingredients slowly until slightly thickened and remove from heat.

Chiffonade ½ pound of sorrel and then sauté it slowly for a couple of minutes in 1 tablespoon of unsalted butter. Remove from the heat and puree along with the cream mixture. Reheat slowly while the cakes are browning.

Fresh Tomato Sauce for Fish Cakes

Ingredients:

4-5 large ripe tomatoes, cored and roughly chopped. Remove skin and seeds if using blender, but a food mill is preferred.

1 tablespoon tomato paste

3 tablespoons olive oil (first cold pressing)

Salt and pepper

1 teaspoon red or white wine vinegar

Optional: chopped parsley/shredded basil

Place the tomatoes and paste in the food mill and strain it into a bowl. Add the rest of the ingredients, finishing with the herbs.

If the cakes are to be the main course, large fresh asparagus cooked until easy to chew and served at room temperature, drizzled with a fine olive oil and shaved Parmesan Reggiano, is nice.

Everything can be done ahead except to brown the cakes and reheat the sauce. Do not forget to have baguettes to clean up the plate.

*   *   *

Now for a baked fish that our cook used to make when we lived in Portugal. We had a small villa way up above the town of Cascais, just outside of Lisbon, on the beautiful west coast of Portugal. It had been a simple fishing village until one day the king came along and decided to summer there. Even so, there was a very large and active fish market by the beach where burly fishermen's wives hawked their husbands' catch as the boats came in, waving their boning knives in the air and calling out for the customers' attention. Cod and sardines were dried and salted right on the beaches, and spiny lobsters were stored in grottos on rocky points where they were kept from being washed out by the tide with steel or wooden bars across the mouth of the caves.

Paella was the plat du jour at the little cafés perilously perched on the rocks between the road and the sea, where you would sit at a little umbrella table and share a pitcher of sangría along with the paella.

Baked Cod, Scrod, Halibut

Ingredients (serves 2):

2 onions thinly sliced

2 medium potatoes sliced ¼ inch thick

2 large cloves of garlic, minced

¼ cup olive oil and vegetable oil mixed, or simply a light olive oil

1 ¼ pound center cut piece of fish

½ cup small black pitted olives halved

½ cup of mixed white wine and tomato sauce

Dried rosemary crumbled and chopped fresh parsley to taste

Salt and pepper.

Preheat oven to 450°F.

Sauté the onions and garlic in half the oil over medium heat until a light golden color. Remove the onion and garlic and set aside. Replace with the potatoes and sauté them until golden. Combine the onions and potatoes off the heat and place them around the fish in a shallow baking dish. Add the seasonings, olives and finally the tomato sauce. Bake in the oven for about twenty minutes or until the fish flakes easily with a fork. Be sure not to overcook the fish.

Letter # 29

SUMMER, 2004

Paris Bistro

Just two years ago this month, I put away an article I had just read which was by one of my very favorite *New York Times* writers, R.W Apple Jr. It was titled "In Paris, Bistros Still Draw a Full House." I took it along when we went to France the first week in May this year and on our second night went to La Grille at 80, rue du Faubourg-Poissonniére, 10e. We had never dined there before, but back in the '80s used to frequent another bistro of the same name. It had a great zinc bar in the front room. When the restaurant closed, we tried very hard, without luck, to find the zinc bar for our house on the Virginia coast.

We followed Mr. Apple's instructions, reserving the banquette in the back of the tiny dining room overseen with great humor by the one waiter, and ordered first a small, very fresh mixed green salad followed by their specialty, turbot, seared and served with a *beurre nantais*, that I cannot find the recipe for anywhere (the closest one, Nantua, has puree of *écrevisses* in it). We also ordered the thin sliced potatoes baked in butter, and to go with this, chose what turned out to be an excellent house Sancerre, not too sweet (Michel, 2001, Domaine Les Beaux Regards), served very cold in frosted glasses. With food you love to eat and a wine you love to drink—on a warm spring evening, enclosed with blood red walls and the cheerfulness of the late daylight through the lace curtained windows—we knew that this was exactly where we wanted to be, right back in the old heart of Paris. On the way out I mentioned to the owner that we had come at the recommendation of Mr. Apple and we were immediately shown the table where he dined two or three times a year with Mr. Sulzberger of *The New York Times*. We told M. Cullerre that Thibaut tutored the Sulzberger children in the years just prior to the war in order to pay his way through Columbia Law School.

Two days later we flew to Prague with its very young population and lovingly restored buildings. We dined well at a restaurant by the name of U Patrona *(www.upatrona.cz)*, in the "Little Quarter", ordering roast goose and venison marinated in Pernod. The wine they recommended was a Chilean Caliterra.

Summer Fruit Desserts

Sautéed Strawberries

Ingredients (serves 6):

5 pints of ripe strawberries hulled

1 ½ teaspoon olive oil

¾ cup of vanilla sugar or regular sugar with a teaspoon of vanilla added

Slice 3 pints of the fruit into six pieces each.

Heat the olive oil until hot, but not smoking, and add the strawberries and ¼ cup of the sugar, stirring constantly for two minutes. Take the pan off the heat and leave the fruit to come down to room temperature. The sauce is better if not served cold.

This sauce can go over ice cream, cake, or on strawberry shortcake. However, strawberry or raspberry sorbet is my favorite, either bought or made at home. This recipe can also be made with peaches.

Strawberry Sorbet

Puree the remaining 2 pints of strawberries in a processor along with 1 cup of water and the remaining sugar until very smooth. Strain the puree and then put it in an ice cream machine and follow the directions given with the machine. Either serve immediately or store in the freezer.

Juliet Romanov Strawberries

Ingredients:

3 cups small strawberries hulled

4 teaspoons fine granulated sugar

⅔ cups sour cream or crème fraîche

3 teaspoons almond flavored liqueur

Place the berries in a sieve over a bowl and pour the sugar over. Chill covered for one hour. With a slotted spoon divide the strawberries between four dessert plates. Whisk the sour cream or crème fraîche into the berry juice remaining in the bowl and then add the almond flavor liqueur. Pour the sauce over the berries.

Gynt's Sherry

The Gainsborough Studios is an old building on Central Park South about a block down from Columbus Circle in Manhattan. The front apartments are studios with two story high great windows facing up the park with an unobstructed north light. On the back side of the buildings are small apartments which were rented out by the artist-owners in the building to help defray the cost of the studios in this high rent district. My former father-in-law owned one of these studios.

Albert "Gynt" Smith, a portrait painter, went off to war with the Essex Troop, a mounted calvary unit from New Jersey, had great good looks and dressed with a style to compliment them. He even wore a tie and jacket of his own design while painting. He took the English smoking jacket and had it copied in felt the color of a pool table and banded around the collar and down the front with simple black braid. He had one in black to wear at home for dinner.

There was always a decanter of sherry on the long refectory table in the studio, behind and above which there hung a monstrous Spanish style painting which had been left there by the previous owner because the window did not open wide enough to lower it to the street. In any case, the sherry was very good. He would take a bottle of Tio Pepe Spanish sherry and then start adding Harvey's Bristol Cream until he liked the balance. I still do this today.

Perfect Combinations

A crisp dry Bordeaux with briny oysters

White Burgundy, Montrachet, Puligny, Chasing, with lobster and melted butter

Dry Spanish Sherry-fino with shrimp sautéed with oil and garlic

Letter # 30

FALL, 2004

On a soft and warm early fall evening Julia Child came for dinner. It was just the three of us, Thibaut, Julia, and I, dining in the little sheltered garden behind our row house in the Georgetown section of Washington. Faced with the thought of cooking for Julia, who was by then a great American culinary personality, I decided, defying good reason, not to serve a French meal but instead a Spanish one. I suspected that if the meal were not French she might not notice my mistakes.

Julia Child on television was the same person who was your friend; everything about her was big and grand: her bones, her size, her heart, her laugh, her lack of self-importance, her loyalty, and of course her sense of fun and the ridiculous.

I put together a favorite recipe for paella taken from *Michel Field's Cooking School*. I forget what we had for dessert because by that time we were into stories and red wine.

Some years later we rented Julia's house outside the village of Plascassier near Valbonne in the south of France. It was a one-floor stone house on a property owned by Simone Beck, who was one of the co-authors with Julia of *Mastering the Art of French Cooking*. Simone insisted that Thibaut escort her to mass each Sunday. She enjoyed talking to a man "en route" down to the little church in the next village. She would give him a critique of all Julia's successes and mistakes, marrying Paul Child being, in her mind anyway, the biggest one. He was her "bête noire" for his often-poor disposition toward Julia and his lack of attention to her co-author. Anyway, after mass there would be lunch down in Mougins at a "two forks" where she claimed the food was superior to the famous "Moulin" up the road. Because of this, she was accorded much deference from the owner and staff.

Julia's house was furnished with odds and ends that she and Paul had picked up along the way, nothing noteworthy except for a set of beautiful green wine glasses and tumblers from Biot. All through the house the walls were hung with rather cheerless paintings by Paul with the most cheerless hung in the pleasant master bedroom. While there we had to sleep in the little guest room off the living room, as the big room was furnished with only a single bed and bureau for Paul, and Julia slept across the hall in a small, short little bed in what could only be called a dressing room.

The kitchen was a generous size, housing about a thousand gadgets filling all the drawers or hanging from hooks on the walls. Pot, pans and sieves climbed the walls in every size imaginable and behind each tool or pan on the wall was a black outline of the utensil executed by Paul so that whatever belonged there could be returned to its rightful place. Everything was out in the open, either hanging or on shelves so that anyone could work there. Off to one side was an old French refrigerator of the standard French miniscule size. The massive black-iron stove was so terrifyingly complicated to light that it needed the caretaker to assist in lighting the oven. An oversize work table was in the center of the kitchen. I was excited to be able to cook in this kitchen-laboratory where Julia Child had mastered the art of French cooking with great exuberance and success.

I miss Julia Child and I miss her for my children and grandchildren who might not have an "Aunt Julia" urging them to come into the kitchen and learn how to stir, mix, measure, beat and serve. Here are some quick tips from Julia:

Frozen Peas

Thaw a 10 ounce package of peas until they can be separated. In a saucepan bring the following ingredients to a boil.

220

Ingredients:

1 tablespoon of butter

1 tablespoon of minced shallots or green onions

¼ teaspoon of salt

A pinch of pepper

½ cup of fresh or canned chicken broth

Add the peas, cover and cook at a low boil for five to six minutes. Uncover the pot and rapidly boil off the remaining liquid.

P.S. I do not remember the last time that I found fresh spring peas in the market.

Vichyssoise á la Russe

Ingredients:

Two 20 ounce cans of vichyssoise (the best you can find), chilled

Salt, pepper and lemon juice

Optional: chicken stock or milk, chilled sour cream as necessary

1 cup canned julienne of beets, drained and seasoned with salt and pepper

2-3 tablespoons finely chopped chives

Pour the cold soup into a bowl and season with salt and pepper, lemon juice. If you prefer a thinner soup dilute with chicken stock or milk. If, however, it is too thin add some sour cream. Chill until serving time.

At the last minute set out six bowls and fill them with the soup. Garnish the soup with a heaping soupspoon of cream or crème fraîche, in the center and top that with another heaping spoonful of beets. Sprinkle the top of the beets with chopped chives or scallion tops.

The Hare

Early one fall, four of us drove down from Paris to visit an old manoir in the Loire Valley region of France. We were on our way to participate in a family shoot followed by ten days on a canal barge taking us from the canal de Nivernais up to Paris. It was a family shoot, so we were the only non-family invitees. We drove up to the house through flower and vegetable gardens into a courtyard where the families were gathering before lunch. We were shown to two bedrooms off the courtyard in which to rest before the shoot and change for dinner later in the evening. There we found lying on each pillow a double-barreled shotgun and on each trigger a small bouquet of flowers from the garden.

Across the courtyard from the front door was a very wonderful, long and high *allée*, perhaps seventy-five feet long arched in the middle and planted with ancient grape vines which had been trained on a wire frame. It was a wonderful place to be shaded from the sun, with soft air filtering through. You felt as though you were walking down the aisle in a green chapel. Here is where we gathered for champagne before lunch, three generations of family and dogs and a large assortment of old green metal garden chairs to sit on.

Lunch was gay and noisy around two tables, a very large round table for the adults. I believe it could seat twenty-four and there was a smaller one next to it for all the children under eighteen.

After a short nap, we returned to the courtyard in the late afternoon, where we were broken up into small groups and sent on our way out into their meticulously kept French fields, while all the children too young to shoot were dispatched to a patch of woods that stood at the edge of the fields. I do not think there is an untended forest in Western Europe, as wood is of such great value. The children were instructed to make as much noise as possible while beating the brush, and this they did by singing nursery songs in high pitched young voices, causing every animal and bird under cover in there to escape out into the fields where we were waiting to shoot them.

The rules of the shoot were simply that anything that moved, except children of course, and was edible, was fair game.

Just before dusk the day's take was laid out in the courtyard with a hare at one end and a little bird at the other. There was something for everyone—and we drew the hare. Champagne followed after a change for dinner. Toward the end of the evening, Le Comte d'Harcourt whispered in my ear that he must disappear for a few moments as he wished to honor the American guests who had become his friends because the two fathers had met and become friends during the war—so he was going down into the cellar to bring up two bottles of his oldest Bordeaux to celebrate the occasion. Two old and dusty bottles were carefully carried in and set on the table by an old maid of the same vintage as the wine. We were each poured a small glass of a vintage prior to 1900 which turned out to still take your breath away, figuratively speaking.

Late that night we left with our hare and the next morning asked the lock keeper, where our boat was waiting for us, if he might be able to skin and dress the animal. He said yes and we also bought late summer vegetables and fruit from his wife. Lock keepers receive very little pay from the government but are provided with a little house and enough land for a good-sized garden. They make ends meet selling their garden vegetables and fruits, along with eggs, or an occasional chicken, to the *péniches* or barges passing through as they offer their help in opening and closing the locks.

We had a lovely girl on board who was taking her culinary training at the Cordon Bleu in London and had signed on for galley duty when my host had contacted her school. She was delighted to be challenged with the skinned and dressed hare and prepared it in a delicious and different way each day until the end of the week when she presented the bits and pieces of leftover meat in a *pâté en croûte*, so wonderful that it is still remembered.

All does not always end well immediately. The next morning as we quietly glided past the d'Harcourt fields on our *péniche*, all the family was down by the canal to wave us good-by. Our enraptured host, and Captain, Alex Mitchell, most nimbly jumped ashore, but in trying to hurtle himself over a post and rail fence like a steeplechase horse, in his haste to embrace the Comte who was running to meet him, fell over the fence and broke his leg. It took two hours to get an ambulance from the village down the field to pick up our host who was lying in the grasses in deep humiliation. He was delivered back to his ship of state, done up in a French cast, further along the canal at the end of the day, and just in time for a saddle of hare served to him in his bunk along with a stiff drink of vodka.

Peach Brandy Glaze for Quail

Ingredients:

1 cup brandy

1 cup peaches peeled, pitted and cut in small pieces or canned or frozen, drained

1 cup apple cider vinegar, salt and pepper to season

Combine brandy and peaches in a stainless steel pot and flame them. When the flame is out add the remaining ingredients.

Use the glaze to brush on roasting quail.

Letter # 31

WINTER, 2005

The ospreys of Boca Grande came back in November this year to survey the hurricane damages to their nests on the platforms that are there by the bridge to this island and have been nesting for some time now. I closely watch one family in particular as I drive back and forth across the bridge, because their platform now sits at a forty-five degree angle and yet they repaired their nest and moved back in, even though it looks like it could slide into the waterway at any moment. There is a perfectly good platform a few yards away but they do not seem to want to give up their old home. Like the people here who just "want to move back in", even while their roofs are still covered with blue plastic and their interiors are covered with creeping mold.

Grating Cheeses

There are three great Italian grating cheeses;

Pecorino Romano—the strongest favored of the three. Pecorino is made from sheep's milk and is made all over Italy, even on the island of Sardinia. Use it in dishes with other strong flavors such as spaghetti with garlic and olive oil.

Parmigiano-Reggiano—made from cow's milk, it is only produced in the area around Parma. The taste is wonderfully earthy. Use it with fettuccini prepared with melted butter. It does not like to sleep in the same bed with the overpowering garlic.

Grana Padano—comes from the Po valley in northern Italy and is a hard grating cheese from cow's milk. It is much less assertive than the Parmigiano so it gets along well married to many other flavors. Grated on asparagus, it lets you still taste the vegetable and yet complements it.

As a first course serve large spears of peeled, cooked fresh asparagus at room temperature, moistened with first cold pressing olive oil and finished with a delicate grating of Grana Padano.

Parmesan Disks

Ingredients:

½ cup unsalted butter

1 cup all purpose flour

1 cup grated Parmigiano-Reggiano

Place all the ingredients in a food processor and pulse just until dough comes together.

Remove the dough, wrap it up in plastic wrap and then roll it on the counter into a log.

Refrigerate for at least two hours.

Heat oven to 325°F

Grease two baking sheets and cut the logs into thin disks while still cold and place on cookie sheets.

Bake twelve to thirteen minutes or just until they start to color.

Remove them from the oven and increase the heat to 500°F.

Return the cookie sheets to the oven for three to four minutes until the disks are golden. Watch them carefully.

Cool on wire racks and store in a covered jar.

I often cut the log in half and freeze one for later use, or the finished crackers can be frozen when cooled.

Parmesan Onion Puffs

Ingredients:

3 tablespoons freshly grated Parmigiano-Reggiano

½ of a small yellow onion, peeled and minced

½ cup of mayonnaise

2 tablespoons of parsley, finely chopped

8 slices of white bread, crust removed and cut into 32 rounds with a 1-inch cookie cutter

The simplest way to do this is to first put the bread rounds on a cookie sheet and bake them for ten to fifteen minutes, without turning, until pale gold. Meanwhile, process small cubes of the parmesan in a mini food processor by pulsing. Remove to a bowl and repeat with the onion and parsley adding them to the bowl and finally adding the mayonnaise, salt and pepper. Mix well

Heat broiler.

Drop a teaspoon of the mixture on each bread round and, just before serving, place under the broiler for about two minutes.

This recipe has been around since the advent of the cocktail party.

When we stayed in the south of France we always rented a house in a village that faces south across the beautiful fertile Plateau du Vaucluse and to les Petites Montagnes du Luberon. If you take a house in the countryside, you are sometimes apt to live in the manner that you live in at home, rather than to be immersed in the culture of the place you have come to. The villages are walled and sit atop the hills within eyesight of each other, and when you pass through the walls, you enter, as a visitor, into another culture to which you must take pains to be respectful. If I go to the butcher and there are people ahead of me I must acknowledge the butcher by saying Monsieur and then his wife, who takes the money, by Madame, followed by acknowledging each person ahead of me in line in the same manner. This form of greeting is very Provencal. The people are extremely polite and pleasant. Even the plumber arriving for his lunch at the "Café de la Poste" gives a greeting as he passes his customers taking their lunch "en plein air."

There is a lovely lady, the widow of an army officer, who lives at the top of the village in the ramparts that belong to the château. Her salon is small but beautifully arranged with antiques that they bought over the years.

They had seriously considered retiring in the countryside of Beirut in Lebanon but in the end returned to France. When she has a small dinner, she puts a long table in the salon where she serves a light meal of three courses, two of which are at room temperature and the last a molded brick of ice cream with sauce.

Some years ago a friend of mine, Carol Cutler, wrote a cookbook entitled *Pâté: The New Main Course for the '80s*. She had lived in Paris while her husband was editor of the *International Herald Tribune*. She studied at the Cordon Blue and l'Ecole de Trois Gourmands in Paris. As she says, "Pâtés are elegant and totally do-ahead—since they *should* be made ahead."

Fish Terrine

Serves 6

The following terrine is best if made two days ahead.

The sauce can be made three days ahead.

Chill the food processor and blade in the freezer.

Ingredients:

6 cup loaf dish or fish mold

1 long carrot cut in half lengthwise

4 scallions including green tops, chopped

2 tablespoons butter plus butter for greasing mold

2 oil-packed anchovy fillets

1 cup heavy cream

10 ounces frozen chopped spinach, defrosted

2-3 pimento halves cut in strips

1 pound fillets of flounder, haddock or cod cut into 1-inch pieces and chilled

2 eggs

2 tablespoons vermouth

2 teaspoons fresh basil or 1 teaspoon dried

1 tablespoon dill

1 teaspoon ground coriander

¼ teaspoon cayenne

2 teaspoons salt and ½ teaspoon white pepper

Cook the carrots in boiling water six to seven minutes. Drain under running cold water, dry, wrap in towel and refrigerate.

Sauté the scallions in butter until soft, not brown.

Cool and chill.

Place anchovy fillets and ¼ cup cream in a pot and bring to a simmer for one minute. Stir until anchovies dissolve. Cool and chill.

Squeeze all water from the spinach. Chill.

Chill pimento strips on toweling

When ingredients are chilled; heat oven to 350°F

Place fish, eggs, anchovy cream, and remaining cream into a cold food processor, puree until smooth and remove to a bowl.

Keep the carrots and pimentos aside.

Process the rest of the ingredients and incorporate into the fish mixture.

Cut parchment paper to fit the top and bottom of the loaf pan.

Butter the loaf pan, place the paper in, butter it and smooth in half the mixture. Add a double row of pimento slices down the center and surround with carrot halves, round side down. Add the rest of the puree, smooth, and bang the mold sharply on the counter. Butter the top paper and place on the terrine. Cover with foil, pierce an air hole in the foil and place in a water bath half way up the mold and bake in the oven for one hour or until it reaches 150°F.

Remove the mold from the oven; remove the foil but leave in the water bath for thirty minutes.

Remove and place weights on top (2 cans of food) for two hours. Refrigerate for one to two days.

Remove from the refrigerator one hour before serving.

Place the bottom of the mold in hot water for several minutes to loosen.

Rosy Cream Sauce

Ingredients:

1 cup sour cream

½ cup tomatoes, peeled, seeds and juice extracted and coarsely chopped

1 tablespoon bitters

Salt and pepper

Process all the ingredients in the blender until smooth.

Bring to room temperature and whisk before serving. It will keep for three days.

Letter # 32

SPRING, 2005

In a letter from Winston Churchill to his brother Jack while at "Hoe Farm," a house rented by the brothers in 1915, he commented that "It is really a delightful valley and the garden gleams with summer jewelry. We live very simply—but with all the essentials of life well understood and well provided for—hot baths, cold champagne, new peas and old brandy."

This quote is from a beautiful and interesting new book entitled *Sir Winston Churchill, His Life and His Paintings* by David Coombs and Mini Churchill. They chronicle his life on one side of the page and show his paintings of that period on the opposite page.

The following recipes come from a letter I received from a dear friend with the beautiful name of Theodosia Burr Martin written in the kitchen at "Knaves Lodge" where she lives on her mountain in the Catskills. Betty and Leslie ran the cooking, serving, and chauffeuring departments for the Martins for many, many years. They were Scots and Betty had learned to cook in the British Army, of all places. Leslie knew how to fold a napkin and would make how-to drawings for me to take home. They loved the Catskills, for it reminded them of Scotland. Many a September day I would visit Betty in the kitchen to see what she was making, especially if she was baking, and to listen to her stories of life in an army kitchen. No Cuisinart for her. In a twinkle of the eye, a mound of flour on the old kitchen table became dough and then a pie plate of the lightest crust. Betty said that the secret of a good crust is to always use part lard. All Betty's recipes called for a "dab" or a "tab" of something.

Guacamole Recipe with Tortilla Chips

Ingredients:

1 jar of Green Mountain Gringo Salsa (mild)

4 ripe avocados, mashed

¼ red onion, finely diced

1 small clove of fresh green garlic finely diced

¼ tablespoon cumin

1 tablespoon Spanish chili powder (or 1 small Jalapeno, seeded and diced)

Salt and pepper to taste

Combine all the ingredients in a steel bowl and refrigerate for several hours. A half hour before serving, adjust salt and pepper and serve with organic tortilla chips.

Betty's Marmalade

Ingredients:

1 can of Hartley's thick-cut Seville oranges purchased from Williams Sonoma

1 lemon squeezed after grating the peel

2 pounds of granulated sugar

1 large navel orange, squeezed

¼ can of water

Bring all together to a boil and then add a square of butter to disperse the broth. Lower the heat and simmer approximately fifteen minutes until thick, then test on a saucer for jelling. If it sets, it's ready. Allow to cool then fill jelly jars (that have been sterilized).

I generally prefer tarts to pies since there is only one crust and, as a result, they are quicker to make. Fresh ripe berries and fruit that are in season and ripe, make a superb tart.

Fresh Fruit Tarts

Do not bake in the shell: strawberries, raspberries, grapes, peaches.

Bake a little in the shell: apples and pears.

Tarte aux Framboises

From *Bistro Cooking* by Patricia Wells.

Pâté Sablée Pastry Dough

1 cup of all purpose flour (not bleached)

6 tablespoons unsalted butter placed in the freezer for fifteen minutes

½ cup of confectioners sugar

⅛ teaspoon salt

1 large egg lightly beaten

1 10 ½-inch black loose-bottomed tart pan

Preheat oven to 375°F.

Put the first four ingredients, flour, butter, sugar, and salt, into a food processor and pulse for about ten seconds until the mixture looks like small crumbs. Add the beaten egg and pulse for about twenty seconds more, but just until the dough begins to hang together—do not let it form a ball. Remove the dough and put it on wax paper and flatten to a disk. Cover your fingers with flour and, working quickly, press the dough all the way up the sides of the shell with just your fingertips. Cover with plastic wrap or foil and refrigerate for a minimum of two to three hours.

Prick the bottom of the shell all over with a fork.

Loosely line the shell with heavy foil, pressing well into edges to prevent shrinking, and then fill with rice for weight and bake about twenty minutes. Remove the foil and rice and bake about twenty minutes more until it colors nicely.

Remove the pastry from the oven and cool for fifteen minutes. Leave oven on.

Filling:

3 large egg yolks beaten with a fork in a bowl

Add and blend

¾ cup of crème fraîche or heavy cream

3 tablespoons sugar

Pour the mixture into the pastry shell.

Carefully place a pint of raspberries one by one on top and then place the tart on the bottom rack in the oven for about fifteen minutes until the filling starts to set. When you take it from the oven, sift confectioner's sugar evenly over the tart and leave to cool on the counter before serving.

You can freeze the unbaked shell in its pan ahead of time and bake it the day you will serve it. Just leave it out to come down to room temperature first.

Tarte au Citron

Prepare the same Pâté Sablée shell as in the recipe above.

Filling:

In a large mixing bowl whisk:

⅔ cup fresh squeezed lemon juice

½ cup sugar

3 tablespoons crème fraîche or heavy cream

Add one at a time:

5 large eggs

Pour the mixture into a baked and cooled Pâté Sablée shell. Bake at 350°F until firm (fifteen to twenty minutes) cool on a rack and serve at room temperature.

You can of course use frozen pie crust dough to save time but the shell will not be as sweet or short.

Letter # 33

FALL, 2005

Just by chance we are here at the "Chalet Suzanne" waiting for the passing of another hurricane across the southeast coast of Florida. It is just over a year since hurricane Charlie, also raced through the Straits of Cuba into the Gulf of Mexico, turning inland at Punta Gorda and hurtling its way up the Peace River and on up the East Coast. It is hot, stiflingly humid, and so still that there is not even a rustle of a tropical breeze through the palms. An American flag is languishing on its pole by the reflecting pool in the turnaround, drooping like the barometric pressure from the weight of the air. The birds have gone somewhere, including the mourning doves, along with bees and butterflies and four-footed animals. It is wise to take note of the signals they send that something is coming and go lie in a safe place when they disappear.

Chez Suzanne is tucked in the rolling landscape of the lake country of Polk County in central Florida. Lake Wales is just south of Orlando in an area of little lakes in the folds of the hills which are covered with mile upon mile of orange groves. It is here at Chez Suzanne that the soups that you find on your market shelves are made in a little factory behind the inn from where they are shipped all over the world. The building is at the edge of a grass runway where old plane enthusiasts fly in from time to time for a meal or reunion. Suzanne's soups even went up to the moon. Both pilot James Irwin on Apollo 15 and the Russian crew on the

Apollo-Soyuz flight that followed chose Suzanne's Romaine Soup for their dinner rendezvous in space.

In the late 1920s it was the dream of Carl Hinshaw Sr. and his friend J. L. Kraft (of the cheese company) to have a fine resort in this lovely landscape, but the plans were derailed by the depression, and the consequential end of the Florida land boom and the tourist industry. As a result, Bertha Hinshaw started a small inn with her three young children, following her husband's sudden death in the early thirties. She put a small sign out on the main highway saying that she welcomed travelers for dinner and the night. As luck would have it, two of her early visitors were Mr. and Mrs. Duncan Hines, who were charmed with the hospitality and added it to a Christmas card list they were making of places to stay and dine on the way to Florida. The list grew into "Duncan Hines Adventures in good Eating" and to his now famous food products company. Chalet Suzanne's inn became known far and wide.

During the Second World War most of the inn burned down and so, after the war, a new one was put together using still existing buildings that were scattered around the property, such as one wing of the old stable, the chicken coop, the servants' quarters, and the old children's playhouse which hung out over the lake and is now the main dining room. The hodge-podge ended up with fourteen floor levels in the main building. Dining room table tops are from ancient decorative tiles that Bertha Hinshaw had collected from among the ancient ruins she had visited during her extensive earlier travels throughout the Middle East.

Then there are the guest room cottages which are clustered together and suggest a Swiss village.

Our pre-hurricane dinner was taken by a window overlooking the lake where dozens of large turtles were bobbing their heads waiting for leftover dinner rolls. An impressive water moccasin threaded his way back and forth among them. The waitresses wore Swiss dirndl dresses. The wine was good and there was shad roe on the menu.

The night outside was black as ink on the walk back to our room where a carafe of sherry and two glasses had been left for us. We were fearful of turning off CNN and not knowing what was coming, so the sounds of wind-blown voices in driving rain squalls filled the room until the electricity went off in the late night.

The northern edge of the storm came bursting through a little after dawn but, even so, a knock on the door around nine o'clock announced that there would be breakfast as usual, because the chef had a gas stove. We were given scrambled eggs with chives and sticky buns by candlelight, served by two ladies in dirndl dresses, along with a view of whitecaps on the lake and howling wind whipping through the trees.

Tennessee Caviar

Tennessee caviar, which we have been sending away for ever since we lived in Washington, comes from the paddle fish that are netted in the Tennessee and other southern rivers. It is a large prehistoric variety of sturgeon with a snout like a canoe paddle and produces an egg that is close in color, size and taste to the sevruga of the Caspian Sea. The hackle-back sturgeon roe, though it is the same size, are black rather than grey. On a speaking trip to Tennessee, Thibaut was introduced to a cousin who was producing caviar and was taken on a tour of the operation. At about the same time, a friend, Selma Roosevelt, chief of protocol at the White House, released to the *Washington Post* the menu for a State Department lunch to be given by George Schultz for Prime Minister Chirac of France. On the all-American menu was "mousse of smoked trout, gravlax and Tennessee caviar." Our ambassador to France at that time was Joe Rogers from Tennessee and he was delighted to showcase his caviar to the French.

Caviar Omelettes

For each serving make a 2-egg omelet, beating with 1 teaspoon water. Season with a pinch of salt and cayenne.

In a skillet heat 1 teaspoon butter until very hot but not brown. Pour in the egg mixture and stir briskly with a fork, shaking the pan all the time. The omelet will set in about one minute (when the fork makes a visible track through the egg). Remove the pan from the heat and put a generous teaspoon of caviar down the middle and fold the omelet in half. Serve with a dish of sour cream or crème fraîche.

Caviar Vinaigrette

Prepare a vinaigrette sauce using a small amount of very fine wine vinegar, combined with a first cold pressing olive oil. Lightly season with salt and pepper. Stir in a generous amount of caviar and serve over plain green salad of either Boston or bibb lettuce.

When you next go to buy a bottle of wine, take a look at the label for the alcoholic content. It can run from 12 to more than 14 percent. That sounds like nothing but it is actually a substantial difference in alcoholic strength. The big American distributors want to increase their wine sales by increasing the alcohol in the wine. It is really better to stay between 12 ½ to 13 ½ percent. You will find that foreign wines have generally not raised their alcoholic levels much, if at all.

The wines suggested below are for everyday drinking, with good quality and an everyday price.

Piper Sonoma Blanc Champagne (This is pleasant champagne).

Chateau de la Chaize-Brouilly (An old favorite from George DuBoeuf).

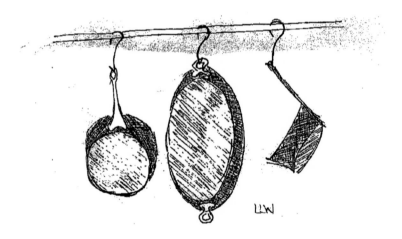

Letter # 34

SPRING, 2006

Indoors or Outdoors

Tomatoes-Cerise's Sauté au Basilic

Ingredients:

1 pound cherry tomatoes (medium size)

1 or 2 garlic cloves

A handful of basil leaves

2 large sprigs Italian (or curly) parsley

¼ cup good olive oil

1 teaspoon sugar

Fresh ground salt and pepper

1 teaspoon thyme leaves

Chop together the garlic, basil and parsley.

Remove stems from the tomatoes and then wash and dry them thoroughly.

Put a skillet on the grill. Heat it and then add the oil and heat until hot but not smoking.

Add the tomatoes, sugar, salt, pepper and stir for a couple of minutes until the skins crack.

Add the garlic mixture and stir for a couple of minutes. Do not let the garlic brown. Serve.

Agneau Marine

Ingredients:

8 lamb chops

3 lemons

Garlic

Salt

Olive oil

Several branches of fennel, a generous amount of fresh sage leaves, oregano, and parsley. (You can substitute with other seasonal herbs and with other meats.)

Place the chops in a deep platter and pour on the lemon juice along with some salt. Coarsely chop the herbs and spread on top. Drizzle olive oil over the meat and marinate for at least three hours in the refrigerator. Wipe off the excess marinade and grill over medium heat, turning and testing, as they cook rapidly. Last night I used fresh rosemary, marjoram, fresh ground sea salt and black pepper with garlic.

Grilled Salmon Steaks with Ginger

Ingredients:

2 ½ pounds of salmon, ¾ to 1 inch thick with skin on.

Melt together:

1 tablespoon of brown sugar

1 teaspoon of honey

2 teaspoons of unsalted butter

Off the heat, whisk in the following ingredients and cool:

2 tablespoons of Dijon mustard

1 tablespoon of soy sauce

1 tablespoon of olive oil

2 teaspoons of fresh grated ginger

Preheat oven to 325°F or grill on low.

Lay the fish, skin side down, on heavy weight foil or in a grilling basket, leaving a ½-inch edge. Brush on the sauce and bake or grill with the top down for twenty-five to thirty minutes.

Napa Valley Hamburgers

For 1 pound of ground steak, use 1 tablespoon of onion juice and 2 tablespoons of heavy cream. Form into 1-inch thick patties and grill quickly over a hot fire so they are crusty on the outside.

The Genealogy of a Wine

"What should you ask of a wine? What is its reason for being?"

That is the question that Edward Behr once asked of a Tuscan vintner and quoted the response in his newsletter, "The Art of Eating":

"Wine, good wine is a photograph of a particular vineyard in a particular region at the end of a certain summer. It's not the portrait of the market or the vintner. A good wine, whatever its level of price, originates in the facts of the vineyard.

But most customers like and demand international-tasting wines. Unhappily for the producers, the wines can't be sold on the basis of the individuality and character of the regions."

Letter # 35

LATE FALL 2006

It was already late in the day when we arrived home from the north and opened the doors to a brilliant light that comes with a setting sun. A southerly came inside too, rippling the curtains in time with the rustling skirts of the palms outside. The sundown trade winds moving through the giant tropical foliage were singing of the coming evening while blowing the oversize pumpkin sun down behind the edge of the sea. When the work of the trade winds from the southern seas was done for the day, we sat with our drinks in the cooler air, and darkness fell, enticing the stars to come out and dance low in the blue velvet sky.

Lunch é Deux

One July, some years ago, we rented a French friend's lovely house in the village of Goult high on a hill looking south across the valley of the Luberon. We took a few days to drive down from Paris, arriving late one afternoon. The main terrace stood at the top of the property with a green garden of lavender and rosemary, among other herbs for their scent and other bushes for their color. Every plant had been trimmed into a round ball. Below that were the orchard terrace and then the swimming pool with giant cedars of Lebanon framing the view. Below that was an old village house that had been turned into a guest house, and below that the eye was drawn across the valley of farmer's fields to the mountains beyond.

The housekeeper had left us a dish for dinner which she later told me was always waiting for the owners when they came by train from Paris.

Jambon avec Endive

Core and halve 2 endives lengthwise per person and then simmer them in chicken stock and water until just tender when pierced with a knife. Remove from the broth and reserve the liquid.

Take a thin slice of good lean ham and roll it around each endive half and place them in a gratin dish.

Make a béchamel sauce using the reserved cooking liquid. For two you would probably use 2 tablespoons butter, 3 tablespoons of flour and 1 ½ to 2 cups of liquid. At the end add a little crème fraîche and some mustard or sour cream.

Pour the sauce over the ham and sprinkle the top with grated gruyere cheese, then brown under the broiler.

If necessary reheat the gratin in the oven before browning.

Côtes de Veau aux herbs

Ingredients (serves 6):

6 large veal chops 1-inch thick

2 tablespoons each butter and oil

Salt and pepper

3 shallots or green onions minced

½ cup dry white wine or vermouth

1 teaspoon mixed chopped basil, thyme and/or tarragon.

½ cup sour cream or crème fraîche

Preheat oven to 325° F.

Dry chops and brown three to four minutes on each side in oil and butter. Remove them to a flameproof casserole.

Pour off most of the fat, then brown the shallots for one minute. Add the wine and herbs and simmer for a few minutes.

Pour the sauce over the chops and heat on top of the stove. Cover the casserole and set in the lower third of the oven for fifteen to twenty minutes. The recipe can be stopped at this point and finished later.

Before serving, slowly reheat the casserole on top of the stove. Remove the chops to a serving plate and add the sour cream to the casserole over low heat, stirring for one minute. Pour over the chops and serve with buttered spinach noodles.

Arugula Salad

Combine fresh baby Arugula with diced firm goat cheese and a vinaigrette dressing. Alternatively, a marinated semi-firm to firm goat cheese can be served alongside, accompanied by a baguette or walnut bread.

To prepare the cheese, place it in a container and cover it with a good olive oil. Fresh herbs and sun-dried tomatoes can also be added. It will keep for a month either on the pantry shelf or in the refrigerator.

M.F.K. Fisher wrote in *The Art of Eating* on the subject of salads served after rather than before the entrée. She cautioned to pay attention to the seasonings that will precede the salad and make sure the dressing is bland enough not to upstage the wine being served. She never used lemon juice when there was wine being taken, but rather a good wine vinegar and a heavy greenish oil from California or Spain. Walnut oil is also delicious.

My preference is a green salad that is all green—save the tomatoes for another kind of salad. By the way, if you have not discovered the "Ugly Tomato," look for it, as they are found mostly during the winter months. They ripen and taste like a summer tomato and are grown in Florida.

Letter # 36

WINTER, 2006

It was not the kind of day to leave the city even though the route led south. The hotel lobby had seemed warm and friendly with the home-style smell of coffee, sounds of toasters popping up and newspaper pages turning.

Just outside the front door was January, 1951, damp, still and frigid. A day for snow before lunch and snow it did as we headed our little Ford sedan south on the highway out of town toward Florida, many days away. As big snows often do, it started with great flakes that covered on contact then melted away. But gradually the flakes sneaked up on us, lying like a white ribbon on the edge of the highway and later resting on the rear window and the windshield wipers.

By lunch time we were a snowball on wheels and the wind picked up, making us almost invisible. By two o'clock there were cars and trucks in trouble all around us, so we decided to take the next exit, which turned out to be a small town called Ravenna, Ohio. It was not much of a town, just large enough to support a modest trucker's inn.

The town plows were beginning to come out as we pulled up to the inn. They were not like big plows used on the highways but old, lighter ones that a poor town buys second-hand and attaches to the front of trucks full of sand. The inn had but one room to give us and that was done by moving out a trucker, and sending him down to the town jail where they had emptied out all the miscreants and recovering drunks and turned the cots over to the truck drivers.

Our room overlooked the main street and was warmed by heat that came out from a rat-a-tat radiator under the window.

Downstairs on the main floor was a cheery small bar along with a few tables that served simple food, presided over by the owner's wife, a personable young woman. We stayed with them for three nights, taking our drinks and meals along with the truckers in this cozy place. Late in the evenings, after their work was done, we would talk, over a nightcap, with the owner and his wife. On our last night, the owner's wife came up to us and explained that they had been given a bottle of champagne some time before, on a wedding anniversary, and had never opened it. In fact they had never tasted champagne. Would we like to share a meal and the bottle with them?

The long-haul trucks had been rolling out all that day and the plow trucks now lay idle with exhaustion beside their snow piles. We sat down with our friends at their table in the quiet of the snowy night and in the warmth of our friendship "popped the bottle."

If you wish to share a "happy hour" with a friend, I suggest that you open a friendly bottle of Domaine Carneros Taittinger, 2001, Brut, from the California Napa Valley. It was very reasonably priced at around $25 and has a nice fresh attitude.

Neighborhoods of New York

From its early telephone days until sometime after the Second World War New York City telephone numbers were preceded by the name of prominent citizens such as Rhinelander (Rh), Atwater (At), Cadwallader, or it could also be a section of the city such as Gramercy Park, Murray Hill or Farragut Square. Sometimes it was something different like Exchange for Wall Street and Fulton for the fish market down near the Battery.

I lived in Eldorado 5 and my friend resided twenty blocks uptown in Butterfield 8. We were a city of neighborhoods then and tended to dine more often than not in our own neighborhoods. As in a Paris Quarter, just about everything to run a household was provided from small shops nearby and nearly all of them delivered to your townhouse or apartment. Intimate little restaurants were often located in the basement of an old town house which had been transformed from the original kitchen after the owner had been forced to vacate the house following the stock market crash of 1929. The restaurant owners knew your name and favorite table, fitting you in if you called late and were a good customer.

Down a few steps, then through the door and into a tiny foyer and coat room, then on past the little bar and straight back, railroad style, was the dining room. More often than not, banquettes lined both sides, with mirrors behind so that every diner could see who was coming in and going out, or catch the eye of the waiter. Often there was a pushcart of desserts. Tables were covered with heavily creased white linen cloths and bud vases, except for a few places like "21 Club" and its famous red checks. Onion Soup Gratinée was almost always on the menu and in summer was replaced with Vichyssoise. Coq au Vin, Boeuf Wellington or Bourgogne, Filet de Sole Amandine were all standbys.

Giovanni's Restaurant

This was a popular place in the forties and fifties. First there was Giovanni himself, short and round and smiling, standing at the top of the stairs to welcome his guests. The restaurant was down the street from the St. Regis Hotel on the way to Madison Avenue on 55th Street. The little waiting bar was downstairs where you entered to the tinkle of the cocktail shaker. When your party was complete you were called upstairs to your table. It was an old house, so dinner was on the parlor level in either the back or front room. Everyone seemed to have their favorite table. Giovanni's was where we celebrated. The food was Italian, light and sophisticated. Antonio would roll around a wonderful cart of antipasti as a first course, including his renowned "Clams Giovanni." Giovanni offered me the recipe.

I remember coming into Grand Central Station from boarding school at Christmas time and my mother taking me and my sister to Giovanni's for lunch. Looking around the rooms filled with the lunchtime crowd, I thought "one thing is for sure, the best looking young businessmen in New York are all having lunch here today."

Thibaut tells me that he had lunch there almost every day—so I was right.

Clams Giovanni

For the garnish:

Soften 1 envelope gelatin in ¼ cup cold water.

Heat 1 pint fat-free chicken broth. Add and whisk in the softened gelatin. Pour into a shallow pan or pie plate and chill.

For the filling:

2 dozen cherrystone clams steamed open in a cup of water. Save the cooking juice.

Remove the clams to a colander placed over a bowl to catch any juice and open, saving the shells.

Put ½ cup of the cooking juice through a fine mesh or cheesecloth and reserve.

Place the clams in a mini food processor and pulse until very fine.

Melt 2 tablespoons butter, add 2 tablespoons fine bread crumbs. Cook slowly one minute. Add the ½ cup strained clam juice and ½ cup light cream. Cook three to four minutes. Add salt, white pepper and a pinch of thyme.

Soften ½ envelope of gelatin in 1 tablespoon cold water and stir until dissolved. Stir this into the clams and chill until a little firmer.

Fill clam shells ¾ full and chill.

The clams can be prepared a day ahead. Serve them on a bed of diced gelatin.

Zabaglione

Ingredients (serves 6):

4 egg yolks

¼ cup superfine sugar

½ cup dry Marsala or champagne

In a heavy-bottomed pot or bowl beat the yolks with a hand mixer until creamy. Place over, not in, barely simmering water, add Marsala and continue beating until it forms a light, soft mass (140°F). Spoon into champagne or martini glasses or place over berries. Serve immediately.

Letter # 37

EARLY SPRING 2007

Invitations to the Waltz

There are memories of wartime New York that I dust off from time to time. In school we had classmate refugees, sent over from Great Britain by families desperate to have their children escape the bombings and stay safe with step-families. In my school, as in others, these children had a profound effect on the classroom, with their lovely way with the English language, extensive vocabulary of words and phrases that had disappeared from our American dialect, and making us aware of the major lifestyle adjustments they were going through and their terrible homesickness at the close of the day. At the end of the war there were English families who believed that their children would have a better life in America and did not send for them, and there were those children who did not want to go back to a now foreign place or family.

We had blackouts in New York; not a sliver of light was allowed to seep out from behind the black window curtains we pulled across at dark. Every square block had a pair of air raid wardens, like town criers, who patrolled their area for obedience. From dusk until dawn our wardens sang out hourly in a lovely Scots brogue, "It's ten o'clock; all is well." Their voices always made my mother, a celebrated freshwater fly fisherman, long for the salmon rivers of Scotland. From time to time she would go to a Scottish dancing club somewhere near Fifty-Ninth Street and Bloomingdales, following the sounds of the bagpipes up the darkened staircase to the welcoming lights of the windowless hall to join in the Highland fling.

During this period we lived on East Fifty-Seventh Street in an eighth floor apartment which allowed us to stay there during the air raid drills until the "all clear" sounded. If you lived above the eighth floor you had to evacuate to the cellar and sit among the washing machines, laundry lines, and storage rooms.

The foyer of our apartment was central and square with six doors leading off it. There were not, however, any windows, so we could keep the lights on during the black-outs. The floor was covered in black linoleum with a ribbon of white around the edge, considered "á la mode" in New York at the time. My sister and I were about ten then and so Mother decided to introduce us to the waltz to keep us from being afraid. She set up the victrola on the Philadelphia tiger maple lowboy in the foyer (it now lives in my front hall), and brought in her record albums of Strauss waltzes. When she put the needle on the record we one-two-thread our blackouts away.

Later, when the lights came on again all over New York, mother was invited to the re-opening night of the "St Regis Roof" with its gorgeous dance floor. She told us that the guests waltzed late into the night with Manhattan sparkling like a diamond tiara outside the great windows.

On the Grill

Swordfish

Prepare a marinade of fresh lemon juice, chopped onion, olive oil and basil and marinate the swordfish for one hour before grilling. Baste the fish every few minutes while grilling, turning only once until done. When a small, pointed knife goes easily through the flesh the fish is ready.

Barbecued Salmon Steaks

Ingredients (serves 4):

½ pound salmon steaks cut 1-inch thick

½ cup dry vermouth

⅓ cup fresh lemon juice

12 tablespoons butter melted and cooled

3 tablespoons chopped chives

1 teaspoon soy sauce

½ teaspoon dried marjoram

½ teaspoon finely chopped garlic

Pepper

Prepare the marinade and let the steaks marinate for an hour. Oil the grill well and grill fish for about five minutes on each side. Brush the steaks from time to time with the remaining marinade.

Boned Leg of Lamb on the Grill

Have a butcher bone and tie a leg of lamb for grilling. For easy handling, run two long metal skewers crossway and two lengthwise through the meat to gather it together for easy handling.

Prepare a marinade of red wine, olive oil, peeled garlic cloves, thyme and rosemary. Let the lamb rest in it for several hours or overnight in the refrigerator. Roast the lamb on the grill with the top down, turn the meat every so often until it reaches an internal temperature of 170°F. Let it rest for fifteen minute before carving. It will continue to cook. Lamb cooked over charcoal can be all crusty on the outside, pink beneath. What a treat.

Grilled Steaks with Anchovy Butter

Ingredients:

2 tablespoons (¼) stick of butter at room temperature

9 anchovy filets

1 large minced shallot

1 teaspoon fresh lemon juice

½ teaspoon lemon peel

Combine all of the above and process in a mini processor. Chill.

Take two New York strip steaks and grill them on medium-high heat until done to your liking. Remove the steaks to two plates and spread with the butter while they are still hot.

Prosecco

Have you ever had a glass of Prosecco? Well you might have if you ever had a Bellini at Harry's Bar in Venice, Italy (www.harrysbarvenezia. com).

In 1948, Giuseppe Cipriani was the head bartender and wanted to invent a cocktail using a puree of white peaches, his favorite fruit. He combined some peach puree with the light, sparkling and fruity Prosecco, which turned out to be a marriage made in heaven. French champagne was found to be too rich for the peaches.

Prosecco is the name of a white grape found in the province of Treviso north of Venice in the Venito region. The best vines are found on the hillsides around Conegliano and Valdobbiadene. The wine is described as clean and fresh with traces of apple peel, pears, maybe grapefruit, with a crisp finish. In a recent blind tasting by *Wine Spectator* three of the top rated wines were not over $15. The alcoholic content is only 11 percent. Lightly sparkled in the champagne method called "Frizzanti" and the fully sparkling called "Spumanti." The very finest Prosecco wines are labeled "Superiore di Cartizze" coming from a small sub-zone and are dryer.

Bellini

Ingredients:

1 ounce white peach puree

5 ounces chilled Prosecco

Measure puree into a champagne flute and add the Prosecco

I have read that Prosecco Frizzante prepares the palate for fine cooking and wine to follow far better than the conventional stronger aperitifs and I agree. Have it for "Happy Hour."

South to the Midi

The TGV now takes you just about anywhere you want to go in France and beyond. We came down from Paris to Avignon in Provence in just three and one half hours where we picked up our car right at the new station and forty-five minutes later we were in Fontvielle. From there it is fifteen minutes from the Roman city of Arles and twenty minutes the other way from St. Remy. We had rented a small suite for a month in the "Mas de la Tour," a nice old house with a large swimming pool (important in July and August). Our rooms were up an outside flight of steps, and breakfast was laid out for the guests on a shaded terrace outside the kitchen. Sometimes we would stop in the village to bring home something to have for supper to be taken in a covered area by the pool since it stayed light until almost ten o'clock in the evening.

Slightly to the east of Fontvielle on Route #17 on the way to Maussane there is a very small village of Paradou where you find the Bistro du Paradou. Go slowly; it is on the north side of the main road in the village.

Le Bistro du Paradou

Inside a long room with glossy mahogany tables a great mahogany bar runs down the length of the room on the far side, and there is a group of very efficient waiters to serve everyone. It is usually only open for dinner and reservations are essential. All the diners get the meal of the evening and it is always very good traditional bistro food.

Bottles of good red wine from the region are already on the tables and so even if you do not speak many words of French you will have a fine meal. There is only one sitting so you can linger for the evening and enjoy the scene. Patricia Wells in her book *Bistro Cooking* gives the recipes for the restaurant's famous Friday "Aioli Monstre" (Salt Cod and Vegetables).

The next village, just a little further east on the same route, is Maussane les Alpilles, with a village square filled with umbrella tables set around a very large fountain and a church behind. It is busy at lunch time with waiters running back and forth between tables and their kitchens across the street.

Some Wines for the Summer

The following list is partly personal and partly from the *Wine Spectator,* "Smart Buys," and the *Wall Street Journal* "Screw Cap."

Kim Crawford Sauvignon Blanc, Marlborough, New Zealand, 2006 Smart Buys and Screw Cap.

Matua Sauvignon Blanc, Marlborough, New Zealand, 2006 Smart Buys.

Chateau St. Michelle Chardonnay, Columbia Valley, Canoe Ridge Estate Smart Buys

Some Reds:

George Duboeuf has again won awards for his 2005 Beaujolais.

It was a fine vintage year for the region. In hot weather, chill slightly. Inexpensive.

Moulin-á-Vent is the most full and luscious.

Brouilly-2005 is one of our favorite house wines.

Julienas-2005, fruity, full, smooth.

Bordeaux

Value from Robert Parker

Chateau Thieuley-2003

Gloria (St. Julien), medium bodied

Letter # 38

A Summer Dinner Menu

Pork Tenderloin with Apricot Mustard Sauce

Ingredients (serves 6):

2 small pork tenderloins totaling 2 pounds

½ cup of coarse mustard

½ cup of apricot jam

¾ teaspoon of fresh ground sea salt

½ teaspoon of fresh ground pepper

1 pound of fresh apricots pitted and quartered

Ahead of time: In a small bowl whisk together the mustard and the jam. Dry the tenderloins with toweling and then rub them with the salt and pepper. Place the meat in a disposable broiler pan to fit their length, leaving space between the two. Baste them all over with 2 tablespoons of the mustard mixture. Cut up the apricots and add them to the remaining mustard mixture, coating them well. Add a little more salt and pepper, then surround the tenderloins with the fruit.

A half hour before dinner, turn on the broiler to high and, when hot, place the meat about 5-6 inches below the broiler. Turn the meat once during the broiling, which should take fifteen to twenty minutes. An instant thermometer should read 145°F. Let the meat rest on a cutting board for a few minutes and then carve into medallions. With a slotted spoon place the apricots around the meat and then spoon some of the sauce on top.

Serve with mashed potatoes or buttered noodles.

For dessert, I put 2 tablespoons of Framboise on each plate, then add a scoop of Italian vanilla sorbet and surround it with fresh raspberries.

Framboise is used to make a Kir or a Kir Royal in place of Cassis. It is lighter, with a beautiful color and a superb raspberry perfume. A little poured in a not-so-great or acidic wine before dinner makes it much more agreeable and digestible.

Sauce Verte

Here's another thought for summertime. The color of the following sauce is lovely against the colors of crabmeat, lobster, and shrimp or chicken. It can also be made a day ahead.

Ingredients:

1 cup of mayonnaise, freshly made if possible, placed in a small bowl

½ cup of coarsely chopped watercress

2 tablespoons of finely chopped dill

¼ cup of finely chopped parsley

2 tablespoons of water

Add the liquid herb mixture to the mayonnaise and stir well. Cover and refrigerate. Makes about 1 ¼ cups.

Bibb Lettuce Salad with Crabmeat
and Green Goddess Dressing

Ingredients:

1 cup mayonnaise

½ cup sour cream

3 tablespoons of fresh lemon juice

1 coarsely chopped clove of garlic

1 tablespoon of anchovy paste

⅓ cup of chopped green onion

⅓ cup of chopped Italian parsley

2 tablespoons of chopped fresh tarragon leaves

2 tablespoons of chopped fresh chives

⅛ teaspoon each of sea salt and freshly ground pepper

Puree in a food processor until creamy and green. Refrigerate for at least eight hours.

Place a large leaf of Bibb lettuce on each of eight salad plates and put a serving of lump crab meat, well picked over, on top and then spoon on the dressing. Garnish with chopped chives.

I thought it would be fun to have an Italian recipe for grilling steak. I found one in a magazine called *Taste of Italy*. This recipe calls for T-bone also known as Porter House steak at least 1 ½ inches thick and enough for four people.

Bistecca Fiorentina

You have the choice of seasoning and then refrigerating the steak for up to twelve hours or seasoning it and leaving at room temperature for an hour.

Place the ingredients listed below in a small food processor and make a fine paste:

Ingredients:

¼ cup of chopped fresh thyme (or 2 tablespoons dried)

4 garlic cloves chopped

1 ½ teaspoons sea salt

Ground black pepper

Enough good olive oil to make a paste

Trim any excess fat from the steaks and slash the edges in several places to prevent curling. Rub both sides of the steaks generously with the paste and wrap them in plastic and leave on the counter or in the refrigerator to season.

The grill heat should be on medium high (350°F). The steaks will take eight to ten minutes over direct heat but move them over to a cooler area if they flare up and then put the top down to finish them.

Wickwire Spiced Game Hens

Preheat oven to 450°F.

Serve at room temperature.

Ingredients:

2 tablespoons cumin seed

3-inch cinnamon stick broken into pieces

10 whole cloves, peeled

¼ cup paprika

¾ teaspoon cayenne

1 teaspoon salt

Grind all the ingredients listed above together in a grinder.

Make a paste of:

3 garlic cloves mashed into a paste

1 tablespoon of lemon zest, chopped fine

2 tablespoons of olive oil

6 game hens

Add 2 tablespoons of the spice mix to the paste and rub all over and inside six game hens. Chill them for two hours or overnight.

Arrange the hens breast side up in two pans and baste with remaining spice mix. Roast in the oven for twenty minutes.

LLW

Letter # 39

WRITINGS AND RECIPES FROM WASHINGTON 2009

This old city still has its southern accent and is a beautiful green garden after all the spring rains. There are flower beds, potted plants and hanging baskets all over town. They decorate the thousands of outdoor restaurants and tend to soften and give a human scale to the masses of new, contemporary architecture along the avenues.

This is a town to be proud of and where even the mayor is now spoken of kindly once in a while. Congress went home to face the music so the double-decker tour buses now command the empty streets.

The Dressing Drink

I am all for the dressing drink. I guess that it is it is not offered much anymore but it is, in fact, a very civilized custom. It started many years ago when the weary houseguest ar¬rived or your husband arrived home from a terrible day at the office, you sent them upstairs to bathe and change with a small glass of something of their choosing. Many a time I pour myself a glass of a white or rosé wine to take while I get ready for the evening. It gives you the same feeling of well be¬ing as finding your bed turned down.

Mark Bittman of the New York Times is one of my favorite food writers because he gives out good tasting recipes that are concisely presented. I tried a fruit pie the other day which I want to offer here. I used peaches and blueberries but other stone fruit and berries work as well. Just adjust the sugar to the sweetness of the fruit.

You will need a 9x13 inch or a deep pie dish. You can buy or make a single pie crust. Bittman's recipe is so easy that I used it.

Stone Fruit Patchwork Pie

Heat oven to 400

Put the following ingredients in a food proc¬essor and process 2 or 3 seconds until just com-bined:

1 cup plus 2 tablespoons of all purpose flour

1/2 teaspoon of salt

1 tablespoon of sugar

Add; 1 stick cold unsalted butter cut in 8 pieces and pulse for 15-20 seconds until just blended. Through the feed tube slowly add ¼ cup ice water until just combined. Remove the dough, cover with plastic, press into a flat disk and then freeze for ten minutes, refrigerate for 2 days or freeze for a few weeks.

3/4 cup plus 2 tablespoons sugar

5 large, large but ripe, firm peaches, peeled and sliced

1 cup blueberries

1 tablespoon of fresh lemon juice

Place the dough on a floured surface and flour the dough as well. Roll the dough out to a 12" round more or less. Now cut wide stripes across and then cut the lengths in half. Do not be too fussy. Place the pastry any way you like over the fruits, brush them with cold water and then sprinkle them with sugar. Bake for 35-40 minutes until the crust is nicely browned. Cool on a wire rack.

The Salad Course

Traditionally, a French menu will place the salad course after the main course and before the cheese or desert course. No wine is poured with the salad but comes after words. In the United States, a salad is often offered to start the meal, but the lemon juice or vinegar does harm to the taste buds, so hold off the serving of wine until the next course. Arti¬chokes do the same thing. Cheese served on the same plate as the salad doesn't help the cheese much either.

I have come across a recipe that would suit perfectly a late fall evening when the walkways are covered with crispy leaves and the kitchen is inviting to come in and get warm. The recipe comes from the Auvergne, in France, a rather lonely area which raises angora goats, and where sheep are raised along with hay.

Daube aux Pruneaux

Serves 10

4 ½ pounds of beef chuck or round roast cut into 2 inch cubes.

1 ½ pounds of carrots cut into 1 ½ inch pieces.

1 pound of medium sized yellow onions, quartered

3 bottles of a robust red wine (but buy 4 in case it is needed or the cook gets thirsty).

Salt and pepper and 1 bay leaf.

¾ of a pound of nice-sized pitted prunes

Put all the ingredients in a big heavy casse¬role and let the wine come to a boil uncovered, and then turn the heat down to very low and leave it alone for three hours. Now add the bay leaf and the salt and pepper and leave it to cool and add some more wine as it should just cover the meat. Refrig¬erate the daube for up to two days.

When you are ready to finish the prepara¬tion, add the prunes, bring the wine to a boil and then lower the heat , cover the casserole and cook slowly for about another hour or until the meat is tender.

Serve this dish with boiled potatoes or but¬tered noodles.

This recipe is adapted from "Château Cuisine" by Anne Willan in "Friends of Vielles Maisons Francaises."

Anne Willan had a wonderful cooking school on the rue de Grenelle in Paris and later bought and moved her school to the prettiest chateau in our family.

Barbara Wickwire of Boca Grande and Pitts¬burg, Pennsylvania, sent me her recipe for this spread.

Shrimp Spread

1 large package of cream cheese

1 can of chopped shrimp, drained and rinsed

2-3 tablespoons of chopped onions

1 tablespoon of butter

Juice of1/2 a lemon

Ketchup (several good squeezes)

Worcestershire

Combine all except the shrimp in a cuisinart and pulse adding the shrimp last so that the mixture does not become too smooth. Freezes beautifully.

Letter # 40

SPRING, 2009

"The voice of the turtle is heard in the land. The green book of the earth is open, and the four winds are turning the leaves: while Nature, chief secretary to the creative Word, sits busy at her inditing of a lovely poem . . ."
—Elizabeth Barrett Browning, *The Book of the Poets*

Baked Stuffed Trout

Ingredients:

1 cleaned and boned trout per person

Bread crumbs

Pecans

Garlic

Salt and pepper

Parsley

In a processor combine the above ingredients to make about ½ a cup of stuffing per trout. Moisten with some melted butter.

Make a package of foil or parchment for each fish and add a little white wine and butter before closing. Be sure to leave some air space.

Place on a cookie sheet in a moderate oven for about twenty minutes and then test one for doneness.

Tarragon is another fine stuffing for trout.

Pea and Lettuce Puree

Ingredients:

8 scallions, chopped

½ stick of salted butter

3 small heads of Boston lettuce chopped

2 tablespoons water

One 10 ounce box of baby frozen peas, thawed or 2 cups shelled (2-2 ½ pounds)

Salt to taste

1 tablespoon fresh lemon juice

2 teaspoons chopped tarragon

Melt the butter in a heavy saucepan; add the scallions and cook covered over medium heat until softened. Add the lettuce and water and just simmer, covered until wilted. Add the peas and simmer uncovered until heated.

Put the contents of the pot into a food processor and run just until it is coarsely chopped. Place the puree into a clean pot. It can be done to this point a day ahead. Reheat and add the lemon juice and tarragon just before serving.

Scarlet Pears

This is an adaptation of a recipe from Paul Grimes who went to the restaurant Chateaubriand in Paris where he saw poached pears of the most intense red color. This, it turned out, came from a beet that is added to the poaching liquid without adding any flavor.

Ingredients:

2 cups of sweet white wine

½ cup orange juice

¼ cup of orange liquor

1 medium beet peeled and sliced

2 teaspoons fresh lemon juice

1 cinnamon stick

2 California bay leaves

3 small firm pears, peeled, cored and halved lengthwise

Bring the wine, beet, sugar, lemon juice, cinnamon and bay leaf to a boil, stirring so that the sugar dissolves and then add the pear and cover with a piece of parchment paper. Simmer until done in about thirty minutes. Transfer the pears to a bowl and strain the juice over them. Let the pears cool for half an hour in the syrup. Remove them to a serving bowl or plated and serve with crème fraíche or whipped cream if desired. This dessert can be prepared the day before and brought back to room temperature.

I have enjoyed our gastronomic travels together and I hope you have too! Let this little story be my final offering:

Annette at "Mère Monique"

One day, the young man said, *I walked into a village of medieval beginnings where two little rivers joined, with each boasting its own bridge. While looking down from one of the two bridges, I saw a small grassy park with some handsome shade trees, a nice little gravel beach, and even a fisherman gently casting his long French fly rod into dark, cool pools that a fish might rest in away from the midday sun.*

He had stopped there to rest and had refreshed himself with a swim and then had gone to a little café facing the park where he purchased a demi-baguette of charcuterie with cheese and mustard, along with a bottle of beer.

Lying on my back with my head on my backpack, I listened to the two little rivers talking to each other—mixing their babble with that of the few other picnickers. While I was lying there a family (a man, his wife and two young children) came into the park with a mule in tow and stopped to picnic near me. They set out lunch on a nearby table, watered the mule and then tethered him in a shady green spot. After lunch I went to talk to the family and they told me that they had come from the north of France and, wishing for a camping vacation, had contacted a stable that rented out mules. All their gear was packed on the mule, even the children, if they became tired. The little family was covering, maybe, 10 km. a day. They stayed at farms where it was possible to pitch a tent and be provided with a hot shower and dinner. The two little children were completely engrossed in leading and feeding the mule.

I stayed and watched them cross the bridge with the youngest taking a nap on the back of the mule nestled amid the supplies with the older boy in charge of the reins.

After a while the young man had gone into the village to find a place to stay. While hiking with his friend they had developed a system for gathering information quickly, stopping by the café, the 'epicerie' and the village square.

We would find a place in no time to wash up and change, return to the now busy café and sit in umbrella shade talking to everyone, especially the girls. We would eat a good dinner at a little restaurant with tablecloths, lingering over our wine, planning the next day, maybe the next year and sometimes we had the presumption to plan the rest of our successful lives. But, we had parted a couple of days before at the train station. I was going to walk for one more week before returning home.

The young man came by a small restaurant with its doors open and with the name "Mère Monique" in bold black letters above the double glass entrance doors. Inside there were two waiters in crisp white shirtsleeves setting the tables for dinner; white cloths inside and blue checkered ones outside. He stood watching their quick and precise movements and in a minute or two the restaurant and its small terrace were dressed for dinner.

I called to one of the waiters, saying that I was looking for a room for the night and asked if he knew of any. He said just a moment, I will go in the kitchen and ask my mother and to please wait right there. While I was waiting, I noticed an old man deftly arranging an armful of late summer flowers in a tall vase on a circular table in the center of the room. He was so absorbed in his work, culling and pinching each flower before adding it to the vase. He was still making adjustments when the waiter returned, followed, I assumed, by his mother. She asked me a little about myself and how long I would be staying. I answered, "two nights," as I would need time to do my laundry and write some letters.

"Oui," she said, "I do have a room upstairs above the restaurant with a bathroom down the hall. I will show it to you and if it is satisfactory, you can pay me in advance and take breakfast with us in the kitchen."

He followed Madame up some stairs at the back of the kitchen to his room which, when the shutters were opened, revealed a view of the street below winding uphill on its way to the church bell tower that could be seen above the rooftops. Dinner was to be taken with the family at ten o'clock after the last meal had been cleared away and the stoves were shut down.

The kitchen was cheerful and, with the back door open, the perfumes of the evening joined with the scents of the kitchen. He learned at dinner that the young waiter's mother owned the restaurant with her in-laws.

After dinner when the old couple had retired to their house behind the garden and the waiters had climbed on their Vespers—hurling themselves down the crooked hill to the river—Annette took down two fresh glasses and poured some wine.

We started a conversation that was to last on and off for a week. She would come to my room without presumption or invitation.

When I left I walked down the hill, only turning back when I again gained the middle of the bridge and looked down at the two little rivers as they met before running off together. I looked back at the village for a long moment but the little street that ran up the hill was too crooked to see the restaurant "Mere Monique."

End

CPSIA information can be obtained at www.ICGtesting.com
Printed in the USA
BVOW031329130612

292572BV00002B/57/P